OECD Green Growth Studies

Environmental Policy Toolkit for SME Greening in EU Eastern Partnership Countries

OECD
BETTER POLICIES FOR BETTER LIVES

This work is published under the responsibility of the Secretary-General of the OECD. The opinions expressed and arguments employed herein do not necessarily reflect the official views of OECD member countries.

This document, as well as any data and any map included herein, are without prejudice to the status of or sovereignty over any territory, to the delimitation of international frontiers and boundaries and to the name of any territory, city or area.

Please cite this publication as:
OECD (2018), *Environmental Policy Toolkit for SME Greening in EU Eastern Partnership Countries*, OECD Green Growth Studies, OECD Publishing, Paris.
http://dx.doi.org/10.1787/9789264293199-en

ISBN 978-92-64-29317-5 (print)
ISBN 978-92-64-29319-9 (PDF)

Series: OECD Green Growth Studies
ISSN 2222-9515 (print)
ISSN 2222-9523 (online)

The statistical data for Israel are supplied by and under the responsibility of the relevant Israeli authorities. The use of such data by the OECD is without prejudice to the status of the Golan Heights, East Jerusalem and Israeli settlements in the West Bank under the terms of international law.

Photo credits: Cover © design by advitam for the OECD.

Corrigenda to OECD publications may be found on line at: *www.oecd.org/about/publishing/corrigenda.htm*.

Foreword

Reducing the environmental impact of small and medium-sized enterprises (SMEs) in both manufacturing and services is a key success factor in greening the economy. At the same time, transitioning to green growth needs to make business sense, and governments have an important role in supporting a context that allows SMEs to seize the opportunities presented by better environmental performance.

The objective of this *Environmental Policy Toolkit for SME Greening* is to help governments in the European Union's Eastern Partnership (EaP) countries (Armenia, Azerbaijan, Belarus, Georgia, Moldova and Ukraine) to design and implement key instruments to promote environmental compliance and green business practices among SMEs, based on existing good practices in EU and other OECD countries. Ministries of Environment and of Economy are the key target audience of this document. Besides these key government stakeholders this document aims to provide guidance for action by business associations as well as non-governmental and academic institutions in EaP countries.

The Toolkit focuses predominantly on environmental policy instruments to promote green behaviour of SMEs. It covers three categories of instruments: regulatory simplification and incentives, information-based tools (which comprise both providing advice and guidance to businesses and providing their customers and the public at large with information about their green practices), as well as financial and economic incentives. These instruments should be complemented by appropriate industrial development, regional development and science and technology policies that lie outside the scope of this Guide. The Toolkit draws on the past OECD analysis on SME-related policies, the extensive work that the EC has done to implement the 2008 Small Business Act for Europe, as well as other relevant literature.

In Part II, the planning and implementation of proposed pilot projects in Armenia, Georgia, Moldova and Ukraine are explored, demonstrating in detail how the guidance in the toolkit can be implemented. While targeting the respective countries, they are also applicable to other EaP countries.

The lead author of this Toolkit was Eugene Mazur of the OECD Environment Directorate. The important contributions of Nataliya Batarina, Vladimir Morozov and Guy Halpern, review and comments by Krzysztof Michalak, and editorial support of Irina Belkahia and Lupita Johanson are gratefully acknowledged.

This document has been developed within the framework of the project "Greening Economies in the Eastern Neighbourhood" (EaP GREEN) funded by the European Union and implemented by the OECD in partnership with the UN Environment, UNIDO and UNECE. The views expressed herein can in no way be taken to reflect the official opinion of the European Union.

Table of contents

Figures

Tables

Boxes

Acronyms

ACFCI	Association of French Chambers of Commerce and Industry
ADB	Asian Development Bank
ADEME	Environment and Energy Management Agency (France)
CSR	Corporate social responsibility
Defra	Department of Environment, Food and Rural Affairs (UK)
DG	Directorate-General
EA	Environment Agency (UK)
EaP	European Union's Eastern Partnership
EaP GREEN	Greening Economies in the Eastern Neighbourhood initiative
EBRD	European Bank for Reconstruction and Development
EC	European Commission
ECAP	Environmental Compliance Assistance Programme
EDTP	Enterprise Development and Training Programme
EEN	Enterprise Europe Network
EIA	Environmental impact assessment
EIB	European Investment Bank
EMAS	Eco-Management and Audit Scheme
EMS	Environmental management system
EPA	Environmental Protection Agency
EPD	Environmental product declarations
EPs	Equator Principles
EU	European Union
FI	Finance institution
GBR	General binding rule
GPP	Green public procurement
IFC	International Finance Corporation
IFI	International finance institution
KfW	German public bank "Kreditanstalt für Wiederaufbau"

KRW	South Korean won
MIA	Environmental Investment Allowance, the Netherlands
NGO	Non-governmental organisation
NIEA	Northern Ireland Environment Agency
ODIMM	Organisation for Small and Medium Enterprises Sector Development (Moldova)
OECD	Organisation for Economic Co-operation and Development
SEPA	Scottish Environment Protection Agency
SME	Small and medium-sized enterprise
SME DNC	SME Development National Center (Armenia)
UK	United Kingdom
UNECE	United Nations Economic Commission for Europe
UNEP	United Nations Environment Programme
UNIDO	United Nations Industrial Development Organization
VAMIL	Arbitrary Depreciation of Environmental Investments, the Netherlands
VIBES	Vision in Business for the Environment of Scotland initiative

Executive summary

Although the individual environmental footprint of small and medium-sized enterprises (SMEs) may be low, they constitute the vast majority of businesses and their aggregate impact is considerable.

Many OECD countries have addressed this challenge by implementing information-based tools and regulatory and economic incentives to encourage SMEs to improve their environmental performance, to comply with regulatory requirements and adopt broader green practices that are beyond what is required by law. However, EU Eastern Partnership (EaP) countries (Armenia, Azerbaijan, Belarus, Georgia, Moldova and Ukraine) have so far given little consideration to the greening of small businesses, and lack the legal, policy and institutional means to enhance the environmental performance of SMEs.

There is a great variety of strategies and instruments that should be used as part of a policy mix to promote environmental compliance and green business practices, including:

- ***regulatory tools***: simplification of regulatory requirements for smes through standardised permits or general binding rules as well as other better regulation initiatives; offering regulatory incentives for the establishment of environmental management systems; moving towards sector-specific strategies for compliance assurance
- ***information-based instruments***: advising individual businesses directly or disseminating guidance on environmental compliance and good practices to a wide audience in the printed and, increasingly, electronic form; introducing sector-specific certifications and eco-labels as well as other environmental recognition awards
- ***economic incentives***: grants, low-interest loans and tax incentives for businesses willing to go beyond compliance and invest in greener technologies; encouraging supply chain pressure from larger companies and exerting it through green public procurement.

Based on the analysis of OECD countries' good practices, this *SME Greening Toolkit* suggests several ways to effectively design and implement these tools with respect to the SME community.

Improving regulation of SMEs with low environmental risk

Replace bespoke environmental permitting with standardised requirements. For specific activities with low environmental risk that are practiced by a large number of operators and employ similar technologies, replacing bespoke environmental permitting with standardised requirements (e.g. general binding rules) can greatly simplify regulation. Rules that require operators to notify or register with the competent environmental authority before engaging in an activity are preferable in terms of the regulator's knowledge of the regulated community and control over its potential environmental impacts.

Ensure collaboration between environmental and non-environmental regulators. Environmental and non-environmental regulators can work together to identify opportunities to reduce duplication in paperwork and conduct joint or delegated inspections in selected sectors. Introducing elements of compliance self-assessment by operators of low-risk facilities (e.g. as part of an environmental management system) can both reduce the administrative burden and improve the efficiency of compliance monitoring.

Take a sectoral approach to outreach. Environmental enforcement authorities should work to strengthen their own staff's capacity to regulate and advise small businesses in specific sectors. Environmental regulations tend to refer to activities rather than sectors. However, businesses, particularly SMEs, respond primarily to messages adapted to their sector. The sectoral approach to outreach is part of a larger customer service perspective that environmental regulators should adopt in their relationship with small businesses.

Providing information, advice and guidance

The right message is crucial for the effectiveness of communication tools. Business benefits of improved environmental performance (in terms of increased efficiency and competitiveness) should be the main "selling point" of environmental outreach to SMEs.

Online outreach need to be complemented by traditional communication channels. Although web-based guidance is a cost-effective communication tool, only a minority of small businesses has rated the internet as their favourite way of receiving environmental information. While in the long term web-based guidance is likely to become the primary source of support for SMEs, in the short and medium term online tools need to be complemented by more traditional instruments such as paper mailings, brochures and workshops.

The instruments of environmental outreach should be tailored to the nature and needs of small businesses. Guidance should be concise and clearly distinguish between legal requirements and good practices in order to avoid excessive efforts by small businesses to achieve compliance. It should contain a simple message about the problem, its solution (step-by-step guidance) and where to go for more information. The most appropriate communication channels are likely to be sector-specific, reflecting the different business models and activities within different sectors. Government bodies, including ministries of economy and environment, should work in partnership with trade associations and business support organisations to elaborate and disseminate environmental guidance, which would add to its credibility.

Non-government actors (including business associations and consulting companies) can provide direct capacity building support to businesses through audits of different aspects of their environmental management, demonstration projects and their follow-up.

Key success factors of capacity building activities include:

- involving multiple public sector organisations and industry associations in programme design, implementation and strategic oversight
- affordability of the support services, which has a major influence on their uptake by SMEs
- consideration of economic impacts of green practices (on companies' profitability, employment, competitiveness, etc.)

- promoting the programme's achievements, including through publicising success as case studies
- using local delivery partners to enable capacity building programmes to gain local knowledge, credibility and accountability
- regular, independent and impartial evaluation.

Recognising green practices

Sector-specific green certification (of business practices) and eco-labelling schemes (for products) can contribute to an increased demand for green business practices. They should be designed in a way that the business benefits to SMEs outweigh both the direct costs in terms of fees that must be paid to obtain certification and the indirect costs of staff time to be spent complying with their requirements. It is important to communicate to a broad audience to raise the recognition of the certification or eco-label, starting at a very early stage of the scheme's development. Trade associations should design marketing and promotional materials which a business could use to display to its customers its "green credentials".

It is important to focus on simple, accessible improvements in management practices. Small businesses face serious obstacles in implementing environmental management systems (EMSs), including a lack of resources, knowledge and technical capacity, high upfront costs, and low public visibility. The challenge is to tailor EMSs, both in terms of their content and delivery, to the particularities of SMEs. With regard to SMEs, EMSs with varying degrees of complexity and low on paperwork as well as sectoral green label schemes are more likely to be attractive to small businesses than formal ISO 14001 certification, which is relatively complex and costly.

Creating financial incentives

As a matter of principle, governments should not provide direct subsidies to businesses for achieving compliance with environmental requirements. Instead, governments may introduce tax privileges (accelerated amortisation, reduced property or corporate taxes) and favourable loan policies through public financial institutions to SMEs willing to invest in green technologies. Such indirect subsidies and free technical assistance to SMEs can help to increase their awareness and secure their initial engagement in green practices. However, given the limited availability of public funding for promoting compliance and green business practices, ***any form of assistance should be time-bound and measurable while a gradual transition toward a fee-based system for technical assistance would improve its long-term sustainability***

Supporting access to green finance

Government authorities should encourage private banks and insurance companies to provide incentives for good environmental performance of small businesses. Banks may require an environmental checklist for loan approval, and insurers may demand a statement of environmental risk identification and control. Banks and insurers can also offer better loan or insurance policy conditions to businesses with green credentials.

Sending right market signals

Governments should exert direct supply chain pressure by developing and implementing green public procurement policies as a way to encourage potential SME suppliers to offer environmentally friendly goods and services. To reach SMEs, government agencies responsible for public procurement should communicate their green purchasing policy to a wide range of stakeholders, including present and future suppliers, service providers or contractors, so that they can take account of the new requirements. Governments should encourage larger firms to form partnerships with smaller suppliers on improving their environmental performance and provide public recognition to those who do so.

Building institutional partnerships

A national government body should take the lead in establishing a network of actors engaged in helping SMEs improve their environmental performance. Environmental authorities have regulatory competency over only part of the SME community, and they are not the primary interlocutors of small businesses. However, in OECD countries they often co-ordinate the efforts of other public and private actors to promote green behaviour of SMEs. In EaP countries, this role is increasingly being assumed by ministries of economy.

Working in partnership with business groups can be particularly useful as many SMEs do not respond to outreach activities conducted by regulatory government agencies due to suspicion and fear. Feedback from businesses groups is extremely useful in developing and improving compliance assistance programmes.

Part I

Policy tools for supporting SME greening

Chapter 1

Greening SMEs: Opportunities and challenges in EaP countries

This chapter discusses the importance of greening SMEs and the opportunities and challenges that it entails. While the environmental impact of individual enterprises may be low, in aggregate their impact is significant. SMEs are also important for green growth as key drivers of eco-innovation and key players in emerging green industries. Reducing the environmental impact of SMEs through achieving and going beyond environmental compliance in both manufacturing and services is a key success factor in greening the economy.

Obstacles are also explored, including the difficulty of SME environmental regulation due to their number and diversity of activities, and the challenges that SMEs face in greening, such as limited capacity to respond to regulation, risk aversion, and access to finance. SMEs are often unaware of business opportunities of green practices, are concerned about short-term financial profitability and reluctant to invest in green technologies, especially given the difficulty in accessing affordable finance.

Definition of SMEs

The legal definition of SMEs varies by country and by industry. In addition to the number of employees, methods used to classify small companies include annual sales (turnover), value of assets and net profit (balance sheet), alone or in a mixed definition. The definition in the European Union (EU) is that an SME is an enterprise of less than 250 employees, with a turnover below EUR 50 million or balance sheet total not exceeding EUR 43 million. A small business is defined as having less than 50 employees with a less than EUR 10 million balance sheet, and a micro-business would have less than 10 employees and less than EUR 2 million balance sheet.

Among EaP countries, the definition of an SME in terms of the number of employees is identical to that of the EU in Armenia, Moldova and Ukraine (in the former two countries the turnover thresholds have been adjusted to the average income levels, which are much lower than in the EU). Belarus defines micro-enterprises as having up to 15 employees, small companies have up to 100 employees, and medium-sized firms up to 250 (there is no turnover criterion). Georgia has set lower thresholds: 20 employees for small enterprises and 100 for medium-sized ones. In Azerbaijan, the thresholds for "small enterprises" (a single category) vary depending on the economic sector: 50 employees in industry, 25 in agriculture, and 10 in services, for example.

At the same time, environmental regulatory regimes are designed around environmental risk and not to address any particular company size. No environmental regulation specifically targets SMEs, instead distinguishing low-risk activities and installations, although regulatory guidance usually keeps in mind particular features of small businesses. Environmental enforcement authorities are not systematically aware of the number of SMEs they regulate and do not collect this information.

It is not easy to define low risk to human health and the environment. Environmental regulators in different countries have very different risk tolerances, driven in part by their mandate and the institutional context. In practice, low-risk installations are usually defined "by exclusion", i.e. as those that are not considered high-risk. Risk assessment criteria typically relate to the environmental hazard of a regulated facility (its complexity in terms of impacts on different environmental media, location with respect to urban and environmentally sensitive areas, volume of pollution releases and potential for accidents) and to its operator's performance (compliance record and environmental management practices). Low-risk installations are generally eligible for a simplified regulatory regime.

The environmental legislation of EaP countries defines an enterprise as having low, medium or high environmental risk depending on their economic activity and potential environmental impact. For example, in Georgia and Belarus economic activities with high environmental impact are defined in relation to the requirement to undergo an environmental impact assessment (EIA). Low environmental impact may also be defined with respect to certain environmental media: in Belarus, no air emission limits are set for low-impact facilities.

This Guide uses the term "SMEs" as a more widely accepted term, particularly in the context of greening the economy and in recognition of the specific regulation and compliance challenges related to small businesses. However, it focuses on those SMEs that are considered by relevant environmental regulators to be low-risk installations.

Role of SMEs in greening the economy

SMEs account for approximately 99% of all enterprises (of which over 90% of enterprises are micro-enterprises) and two-thirds of employment across the OECD area. Although small businesses' individual environmental footprint may be low, their aggregate impact can, in some respects, exceed that of large businesses. For example, SMEs account for 60-70% of industrial pollution in Europe (Miller, 2011). The key sectors where SMEs have a significant environment impact include livestock farming, construction, metal finishing, waste treatment, food and drink industry, and textile and leather manufacturing.

SMEs are important for green growth as key drivers of eco-innovation and key players in emerging green industries. Growing opportunities exist in the services associated with greener manufacturing. Highly creative and innovative SMEs in the service industry, such as design and architecture firms or bio-energy solution providers, contribute increasingly to eco-innovation across a broad range of industries. New and young firms are particularly important for radical green innovations, as they often exploit technological or commercial opportunities which have been neglected by more established companies or even challenge the business models of existing firms.

The "green transformation" is also a significant business opportunity for SMEs themselves as important suppliers of goods and services. Indeed, the principal drivers for SMEs to adopt green practices are non-regulatory and include:

- the rising price of commodities and key raw materials
- potential cost savings and competitive advantage
- market pressure from customers.

However, the willingness and capability of SMEs to adopt sustainable practices and seize green business opportunities generally face size-related resource constraints, skill deficit and knowledge limitations. SMEs are often unaware of many financially attractive opportunities for environmental improvement. There is a widespread misperception that protecting the environment is associated with technical complexity, burdens and costs. Even when they are aware of the potential of better environmental performance to improve a firm's competitiveness, a lack of appropriate skills and expertise commonly prevents firms from acting upon win-win opportunities. At the same time, the lack of resources often leads to SMEs being risk-averse and less willing to invest in new technologies, partly because of the uncertainly about the payback period.

The UK Carbon Trust poll found that 65% of consumers want to purchase products from environmentally responsible companies. Yet more than half of SMEs see a greener economy as a threat, about half of small businesses believe that benefitting from the green economy requires a lot of investment capital, and only 22% think that investing in green products and services will lead to higher profits (Carbon Trust, 2011).

For SMEs, going green is largely a voluntary action dependent upon the vision and conviction of one or a few individuals. Many SMEs are willing to invest in more energy-efficient and environmentally friendly processes, but they require reliable partners in financing their investments and the right regulatory framework. However, they often face obstacles in getting access to finance, with banks being reluctant to fund such investments and lacking the specialised staff needed to evaluate SME projects.

An increasing number of business associations in OECD countries are asking their governments to provide support to SMEs in the transition to the green economy. In response to this, the EU has undertaken a number of policy initiatives to support the green transformation of SMEs (Box 1.1), aimed at making sure that regulations are easy to understand and take account of the needs of small businesses; providing clearer information on the range of green choices available and their practical and financial aspects; and using financial incentives to give small businesses confidence to invest in green technologies and management systems.

Box 1.1. **Policy initiatives for SME greening in the EU**

The concerns of small businesses have become a priority as governments across the EU introduce better regulation initiatives. The Small Business Act for Europe (2008) was developed to establish the "Think Small First" approach to policy making and regulation and to promote SMEs' growth. One of its ten high-profile principles is "enable SMEs to turn environmental challenges into opportunities" – a paradigm which lies at the heart of the transition to green growth. The European Commission has committed itself to "rigorously assessing the impact of forthcoming legislation and administrative initiatives on SMEs ("SME test") and taking relevant results into account when designing proposals".

The European Commission has recently prepared a Green Action Plan for SMEs, which aims to:

- Improve resource efficiency of European SMEs;
- Support green entrepreneurship;
- Exploit the opportunities of greener value (supply) chains; and
- Facilitate market access for green SMEs.

Sources : EC (2014), *Green Action Plan for SMEs: Enabling SMEs to turn environmental challenges into business opportunities*, http://ec.europa.eu/growth/smes/business-friendly-environment/green-action-plan/; EC (2008), *Think Small First – A "Small Business Act" for Europe*, https://ec.europa.eu/growth/smes/business-friendly-environment/small-business-act_en.

Obstacles to improving environmental performance of SMEs

Recent research has shown that while SMEs account for approximately 64% of the industrial pollution in the EU, only very few of them proactively engage in actions to reduce their environmental impact: 3-4% of micro-businesses, 7-8% of small companies and 6-7% of medium-sized companies (Calogirou et al., 2010).

For the government, the environmental regulation of SMEs represents a major challenge due to the diversity of SMEs' activities and respective environmental issues, the substantial number of operators, and the lack of information available to the regulator about their levels of compliance. The majority of SMEs are "vulnerably compliant" (EC, 2002), in the sense that they do not know enough about environmental requirements to ensure that they always comply with all of them.

What motivates SMEs and their owners is likely to be very different from what motivates large corporations. Despite their heterogeneity, SMEs have many common characteristics that influence their approach to environmental issues and the implementation of green practices; both in achieving and going beyond compliance (see also Table 1.1):

- Ownership and management are concentrated on the same hands. The entrepreneur plays a key role in the enterprise and his personal preference is usually the most influential factor when deciding about investments and business strategies.

- This entrepreneur is very likely to suffer from important time and task pressure, which leaves him with little time to reflect strategically on future activities beyond the core business of the company. This could imply that investments that are not related to core business are regarded as secondary and suffer from insufficient attention.
- SMEs have a limited capacity (lack of resources, time and expertise) to absorb environmental requirements and to comply with them, as well as a low awareness of the need to address their environmental impacts.
- The entrepreneur himself usually is not well informed about opportunities of the relevant green practices, their costs and benefits. Given this time and task pressure, SMEs usually rely heavily on the opinion of their professional surrounding (trade associations, suppliers, clients, accountants, etc.), which often have the same lack of information.
- The entrepreneur is often risk-averse given the relatively small economic size of the enterprise. Uncertainty may be associated with operational issues within companies, such as the capacity to absorb and implement the change required to improve environmental performance. These include uncertainty about the most appropriate technology to be used and the lack of knowledge on how to incorporate green practices into the core business planning.
- The required pay-back for new investments is often as short as two-three years (it is also a function of the cost of capital). Generally, environmental technologies encompass higher costs in the short term whereas the extra benefits are realised in the longer term, which hinders their adoption by SMEs. Limited access to finance is also a key limitation. The most common environmental issues for SMEs, such as resource and energy savings, which usually are not related to the core business of the company, are only addressed if actions are likely to result in a substantial cost reduction in the short term.

Table 1.1. **Internal barriers in SMEs that prevent the adoption of environmental improvements**

Resources	Attitudes and company culture	Awareness
• Lack of time to investigate issues or locate support or tools	• Belief that SMEs have a low environmental impact and have no environmental issues to consider	• Low awareness of environmental legislation
• Severe time pressure in small enterprises	• Mismatch between beliefs and actions: positive attitude toward the environment is not translated into actions	• Low awareness of support organisations and information sources
• Lack of resource allocation to address environmental issues	• Perception that environment has no relevance to the business: environment given no status as a business issue	
• Lack of investment in training	• Scepticism about the potential cost savings and market benefits	
• Cost constraints on investment	• Prevalence of short-term business planning; belief that costs of environmental measures arise quickly while benefits accrue slowly	
• No employee allocated responsibility for environmental issues		

Source: EC (2002), *European SMEs and social and environmental responsibility,* https://publications.europa.eu/en/publication-detail/-/publication/60177f21-1835-4c5e-bf29-6a47b5b0808f/language-en.

- SMEs experience little external pressure to behave in a more environmentally friendly manner. It is difficult for NGOs or customers to assign specific negative environmental consequences to one or more SMEs, while it is much easier to target large well known enterprises. Furthermore, governments in general avoid increasing external pressure on SMEs by environmental legislation.

A Eurobarometer survey of EU SMEs (EC, 2013) looked at reasons for inaction on resource efficiency. Approximately 26% of European SMEs said that administrative or legal procedures were complex, and 24% said that the cost of environmental actions was a barrier. In addition, 20% indicated that they were hampered by a lack of specific environmental expertise, and 17% experienced problems in choosing the right actions for the company.

Half of SMEs in the EU (51%) do not wish to go beyond compliance with applicable regulatory requirements, while 22% are contemplating doing more than required by the legislation, and 19% are doing so already (for 11% of respondents, environmental concerns are part of the company's priority objectives). The larger the SMEs, the more likely it is to define environmental concerns as a priority.

In similar surveys in EaP countries,[1] among the key obstacles to engaging in green practices SMEs quote costs and poor access to finance (for all sizes of SMEs), and various bureaucratic barriers such as complex administrative procedures and obsolete technical requirements (Figure 1.1). The lack of environmental skills is generally not considered to be an important gap: as other survey responses illustrate, SMEs in the region see themselves as technically competent to introduce green practices. A large percentage of respondents indicate that they do not encounter any difficulties in trying to undertake environmentally friendly actions. However, they still do not want to go beyond compliance with environmental requirements: for about 35-40% of SMEs in Armenia, Georgia and Ukraine this is not a priority for the company.

Figure 1.1. **Barriers to green practices among SMEs in EaP countries, percentage of respondents**

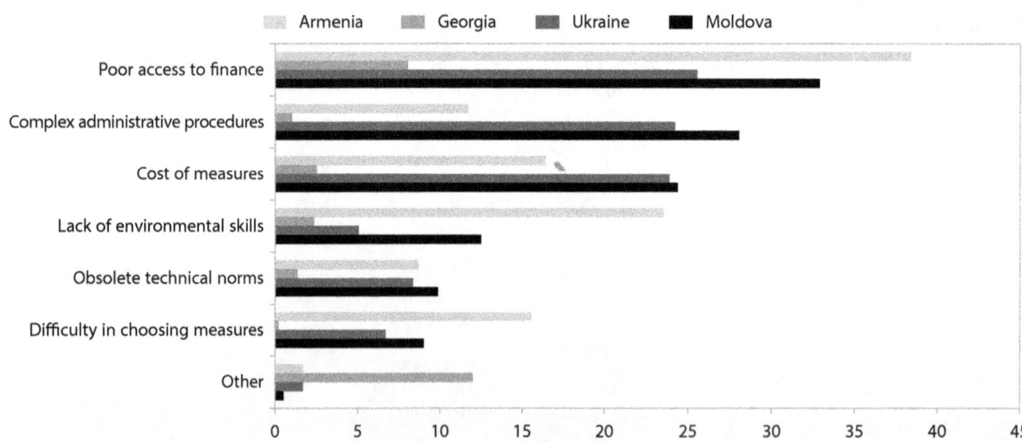

Sources: OECD (2016a), *Promoting better environmental performance of small and medium-sized enterprises in Ukraine*, www.oecd.org/env/outreach/Ukraine%20pilot%20project%20report%20EN.pdf; OECD (2016b), *Promoting better environmental performance of small and medium-sized enterprises in Georgia*, www.oecd.org/env/outreach/Georgia%20pilot%20project%20report%20final%20EN.pdf; OECD (2015a), *Promoting better environmental performance of small and medium-sized enterprises in Armenia*, www.oecd.org/environment/outreach/SME-greening-country-pilot-report-Armenia-en.pdf; OECD (2015b), *Promoting better environmental performance of small and medium-sized enterprises in Moldova*, www.oecd.org/environment/outreach/Binder%20English.pdf.

Conclusion

Reducing the environmental impact of SMEs through achieving and going beyond environmental compliance in both products and services is a key success factor in greening economies in EaP countries. SMEs have significant environmental impact in aggregate and are a vital channel for the development of innovative green products and services. At the same time, there are substantial obstacles which must be overcome to achieve these goals. As discussed during the this chapter, these obstacles are multi-faceted and exist across a range of terrain, including the capacity of SMEs to justify and adopt green practices, the availability of information, resources, and finance, and the capacity and co-ordination of public and private sector actors. The following chapters in this Toolkit explores these questions, and provides guidance supported by good practice from other jurisdictions.

Note

1. The surveys were conducted in 2014-15 in Armenia, Georgia, Moldova and Ukraine using a questionnaire inspired by the Eurobarometer and covered over 400 SMEs in each country (OECD, 2015a, b; OECD, 2016a, b).

References

Calogirou C. et al. (2010), *SMEs and the environment in the European Union*, PLANET S.A. and Danish Technological Institute, published by European Commission, DG Enterprise and Industry, https://ec.europa.eu/docsroom/documents/13176/attachments/1/translations/en/renditions/pdf.

Carbon Trust (2011), *Green Your Business for Growth*, Management Guide, Carbon Trust, www.carbontrust.co.uk/publications.

Miller, K. et al. (2011), *First Assessment of the Environmental Assistance Programme for SMEs (ECAP)*, Final report, prepared by AEA Technology Plc. for the European Commission, DG Environmental and Climate Action, London, http://ec.europa.eu/environment/archives/sme/pdf/First%20assessemnt%20of%20the%20ECAP%20for%20SMEs.pdf.

EC (2008), *Think Small First – A "Small Business Act" for Europe*, Communication from the Commission to the Council, the European Parliament, the European Economic and Social Committee and the Committee of the Regions, COM(2008) 394 final, Brussels, https://ec.europa.eu/growth/smes/business-friendly-environment/small-business-act_en.

EC (2002), *European SMEs and social and environmental responsibility*, Observatory of European SMEs, No. 4, European Commission, Brussels, https://publications.europa.eu/en/publication-detail/-/publication/60177f21-1835-4c5e-bf29-6a47b5b0808f/language-en.

Ecorys (2012), *Study on Incentives Driving Improvement of Environmental Performance of Companies*, Final Report, Ecorys Nederland BV, Rotterdam, ec.europa.eu/environment/pubs/pdf/Incentives_Ecorys.pdf.

Ecotec (2000), *Report on SMEs and the Environment*, Final Report for the European Commission, DG Environment, Ecotec Research and Consulting, Brussels.

OECD (2016a), *Promoting better environmental performance of small and medium-sized enterprises in Ukraine*, Pilot project report, Organisation for Economic Co-operation and Development, Paris, www.oecd.org/env/outreach/Ukraine%20pilot%20project%20report%20EN.pdf.

OECD (2016b), *Promoting better environmental performance of small and medium-sized enterprises in Georgia*, Pilot project report, Organisation for Economic Co-operation and Development, Paris, www.oecd.org/env/outreach/Georgia%20pilot%20project%20report%20final%20EN.pdf.

OECD (2015a), *Promoting better environmental performance of small and medium-sized enterprises in Armenia*, Pilot project report, Greening Economies in the Eastern Neighbourhood programme, Organisation for Economic Co-operation and Development, Paris, www.oecd.org/environment/outreach/SME-greening-country-pilot-report-Armenia-en.pdf.

OECD (2015b), *Promoting better environmental performance of small and medium-sized enterprises in Moldova*, Pilot project report, Greening Economies in the Eastern Neighbourhood programme, Organisation for Economic Co-operation and Development, Paris, www.oecd.org/environment/outreach/Binder%20English.pdf.

Chapter 2

Environmental compliance progress and challenges for SMEs in EaP countries

This chapter looks at the challenges facing EaP countries on greening SMEs, and the progress that has been made so far. It begins with an examination of existing regulatory regimes in EaP countries, highlighting ongoing proposals to move away from uniform application of single-medium permitting. The chapter examines some of the environmental considerations that have been introduced into strategic documents from EaP countries on SME support activities, and highlights survey data on how SMEs are informed about regulatory requirements. The chapter notes that EaP SMEs that do undertake efficiency measures mostly do so for economic reasons. The importance of shifting to new regulatory regimes that lessen enterprises' regulatory burden and are calibrated based on the level of environmental risk is highlighted. In conjunction with that, policy gaps in EaP countries are explored, in particular around technical and financial support for green practices, and effective communication and information tools.

Regulatory regimes

In all EaP countries, the same regime for setting environmental requirements applies regardless of the facility's level of environmental risk, creating a heavy administrative burden for SMEs as well as for regulators. The regulatory systems are dominated by single-medium permitting (for air emissions, wastewater discharges and waste disposal) which applies to every enterprise which has respective environmental impacts. Where general binding rules ("technical regulations") with environmental norms exist, they are not sector-specific and do not distinguish between facilities with different levels of impact.

However, the situation is starting to change as environmental regulators are starting to focus their efforts on higher risk enterprises. For example, Armenia is taking a first step in the diversification of environmental regulatory regimes: the draft law "On environmental impact assessment and expertise" envisages the classification of regulated entities into three categories (A, B and C) with different assessment procedures for each category. Armenia is also developing a law on environmental self-monitoring which would differentiate self-monitoring and self-reporting requirements based on the operator's environmental impact. Likewise, in Ukraine only operators with higher environmental impact are subject to air emissions self-monitoring and self-reporting.

In Azerbaijan, the draft new Law on Environmental Impact Assessment the differentiation of permitting requirements for enterprises based on their environmental impact, sector and type of economic activity. In Georgia, the regulatory reforms made during 2004-07 significantly simplified the administrative procedures for all enterprises, including SMEs, by drastically cutting the number of licences and permits, reducing the licence determination period to less than a month, and introducing "one-stop shopping" for all permits and licences.

Other EaP countries are also planning to take similar measures. Moldova's Small and Medium Enterprise Sector Development Strategy for 2012-2020 envisages adjusting the regulatory framework to match SME needs. Belarus's National Strategy on Environmental Permitting for 2009-2020 provides for the simplification of the administrative procedures related to environmental permitting of enterprises with low environmental impact by 2015.

Environment ministries and their associate institutions provide regulatory information to the regulated community. Specialised environmental information centres, usually associated with environment ministries, provide assistance in understanding environmental requirements through telephone advice, workshops, and guidelines. For example, in Georgia, the Ministry of Environment and Natural Resources Protection has set up an Environmental Information and Education Centre in 2010 to provide compliance advisory services to companies and individuals. A similar Environmental Information Centre exists within Moldova's Ministry of Environment. However, these information services rarely reach smaller businesses.

When asked how they learn about environmental requirements, over 50% of SMEs in four EaP countries that have environment-related permits indicated direct contact with environmental inspectors during their site visits as a key source of regulatory information (Figure 2.1). This means that businesses realised that they had to comply with certain requirements when they were already inspected for compliance. Less than 20% of respondents rely on information provided through workshops or electronically by relevant business associations, while many more (from 16% in Armenia to 42% in Moldova) draw it from the Internet.

Figure 2.1. **How SMEs learn about environmental requirements, percentage of respondents**

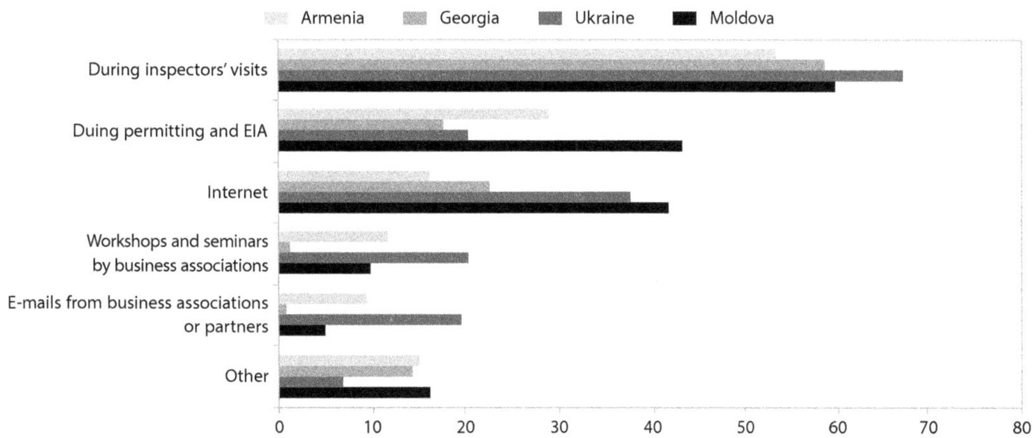

Sources: OECD (2016a), *Promoting better environmental performance of small and medium-sized enterprises in Ukraine*, www.oecd.org/env/outreach/Ukraine%20pilot%20project%20report%20EN.pdf; OECD (2016b), *Promoting better environmental performance of small and medium-sized enterprises in Georgia*, www.oecd.org/env/outreach/Georgia%20pilot%20project%20report%20final%20EN.pdf; OECD (2015a), *Promoting better environmental performance of small and medium-sized enterprises in Armenia*, www.oecd.org/environment/outreach/SME-greening-country-pilot-report-Armenia-en.pdf; OECD (2015b), *Promoting better environmental performance of small and medium-sized enterprises in Moldova*, www.oecd.org/environment/outreach/Binder%20English.pdf.

The differentiation of compliance monitoring regimes is also affecting SMEs. In some EaP countries, the frequency of environmental inspections has been differentiated between broad risk categories. For instance, Armenia is implementing a risk-based system of compliance monitoring. The 2011 amendments to the Law on "Organising and carrying out inspections in the Republic of Armenia" (No. 60 of 2000) and Government Decree No. 1562-N of 2012 stipulated that the frequency of inspections should be based on the assessed level of the enterprise's environmental risk. The level of risk is determined through a scoring system taking into account the enterprise's sector-specific and individual risks. The inspection frequency for low-risk facilities is set at once every five years.

Existing policy incentives

EaP countries have generally given little consideration to the greening of small businesses, and lack the legal, policy and institutional means to enhance the environmental performance of SMEs.

There are a few examples of regulatory incentives for getting certified to an environmental management system (e.g. in Azerbaijan and Belarus). In Belarus, companies deploying an EMS certified in accordance ISO 14001, benefit from financial incentives when calculating environmental tax on air emissions, wastewater discharges and waste disposal. Overall, however, compliance promotion activities are underdeveloped in EaP countries.

At the same time, governments in EaP countries increasingly realise the importance of SME support policies in the context of greening the economy. Ministries of Economy in both Moldova and Armenia are planning to introduce environmental considerations into their strategic documents on SME support activities, but have not yet started the development of specific policy measures.

When a strategy does not have institutional ownership, it is likely to remain a dead letter. In Georgia, a "Green Business Support Strategy for Georgian Private Business Organizations" was developed in 2011 by the Georgian Entrepreneurs Confederation with support from the German government. It recommended establishing an "Information centre for green business", promoting environmental management systems, disseminating of best practices, developing appropriate financing instruments, etc., but has been implemented only partly. The Georgian Green Business Award was announced by the Ministry of Environment and Natural Resources Protection in October 2013. The award is made in the green company, green product and green building categories and seeks to raise motivation of entrepreneurs in environment protection and social responsibility. However, many other policy tools are still lacking.

All EaP countries except Georgia have extensive pollution tax/charge schemes covering dozens of pollutants. These taxes are payable by all enterprises with respective pollution releases, but the tax rates are too low to provide desired incentives for environmental improvements. All EaP countries impose taxes on environmentally harmful products (such as motor fuels and vehicles), but only several of them (notably Armenia and Moldova) have product taxes mandated by environmental legislation. The environmental incentive impact of these product taxes is equally negligible.

Current implementation of green practices

According to the Eurobarometer, over 90% of SMEs in the EU are taking at least some actions to be more resource-efficient. Most common actions relate to minimising waste, saving energy and raw materials. A similar situation can be observed in EaP countries. Despite the lack of government incentives, the vast majority of the surveyed SMEs undertake some resource efficiency measures, mostly to save energy, water or raw materials, or plan to do so in the future (Figure 2.2).

Figure 2.2. **Resource efficiency actions undertaken by SMEs in EaP countries, percentage of respondents**

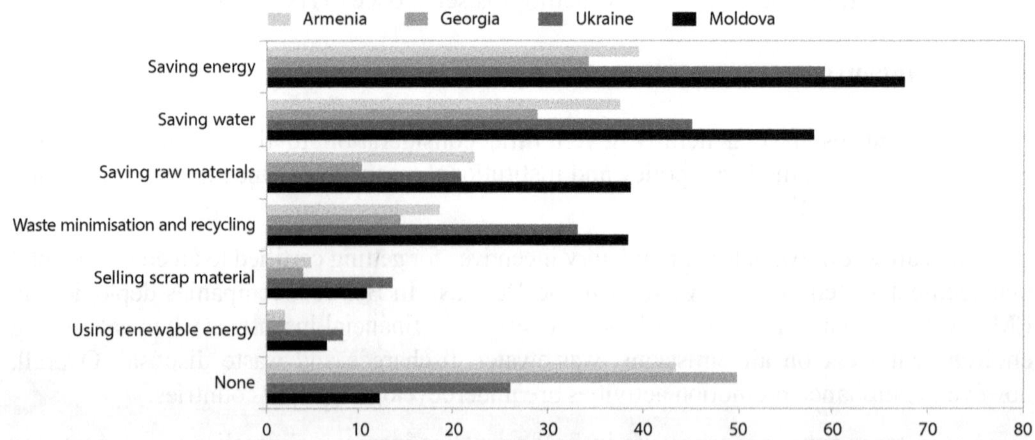

Sources: OECD (2016a), *Promoting better environmental performance of small and medium-sized enterprises in Ukraine*, www.oecd.org/env/outreach/Ukraine%20pilot%20project%20report%20EN.pdf; OECD (2016b), *Promoting better environmental performance of small and medium-sized enterprises in Georgia*, www.oecd.org/env/outreach/Georgia%20pilot%20project%20report%20final%20EN.pdf; OECD (2015a), *Promoting better environmental performance of small and medium-sized enterprises in Armenia*, www.oecd.org/environment/outreach/SME-greening-country-pilot-report-Armenia-en.pdf; OECD (2015b), *Promoting better environmental performance of small and medium-sized enterprises in Moldova*, www.oecd.org/environment/outreach/Binder%20English.pdf.

The main driver for such actions is purely economic: businesses already experience and anticipate further increases of prices of these resources, which is reflected in over 80% of the survey responses in Armenia and Ukraine (Figure 2.3). The smaller the business, the more it feels the impact of resource price changes. Almost 40% of Moldovan SMEs actively pursuing resource efficiency see this as an opportunity to gain a competitive advantage. Environmental awareness, making it a priority for the company, is also a significant factor, especially among medium-sized companies.

Very few SMEs in EaP countries have a certified ISO 14001 EMS, with some opting for a less onerous national environmental management standard. Many of those businesses quote commercial reasons for doing so: for example, in Ukraine it is demand from suppliers and customers (42.3%) as well as efforts to improve the company's image in the eyes of clients, business partners or the general public (26.9%). Almost 30% of surveyed Ukrainian SMEs see an EMS as a useful management tool to improve the company's performance (OECD, 2016a).

The majority of SMEs which have not adopted any EMS signal a variety of barriers, pointing to the lack of capacity, excessive time and cost burden of EMS implementation. Above all, there is a lack of information about EMSs and their advantages, which contributes to the uncertainty regarding market benefits of investing into an EMS. The lack of domestic demand and high certification and implementation costs also play a role in dissuading SMEs from seeking EMS certification.

Figure 2.3. **Reasons to undertake resource efficiency measures, percentage of respondents**

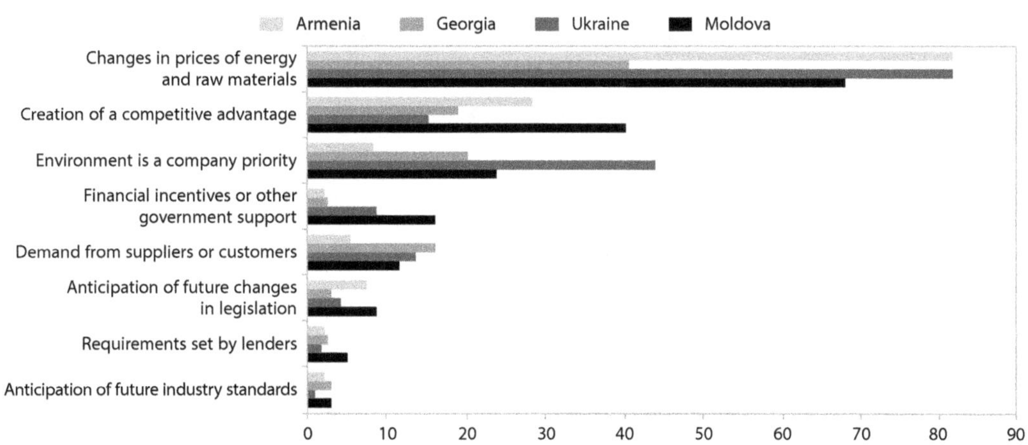

Sources: OECD (2016a), *Promoting better environmental performance of small and medium-sized enterprises in Ukraine*, www.oecd.org/env/outreach/Ukraine%20pilot%20project%20report%20EN.pdf; OECD (2016b), *Promoting better environmental performance of small and medium-sized enterprises in Georgia*, www.oecd.org/env/outreach/Georgia%20pilot%20project%20report%20final%20EN.pdf; OECD (2015a), *Promoting better environmental performance of small and medium-sized enterprises in Armenia*, www.oecd.org/environment/outreach/SME-greening-country-pilot-report-Armenia-en.pdf; OECD (2015b), *Promoting better environmental performance of small and medium-sized enterprises in Moldova*, www.oecd.org/environment/outreach/Binder%20English.pdf.

Technical and financial support for green practices

The situation with government support for SMEs in EaP countries is still very patchy. Governments most often play a passive role in promoting environmental sustainability and best practices and their involvement is generally limited to hosting international donor-funded projects.

Ministries of economy in several EaP countries implement various information and training programmes for small businesses, but they rarely get institutionalised. A positive example can be found in Georgia, where the Ministry of Economy and Sustainable Development has been providing private companies with reliable and actionable industry data and analysis, and making them aware of opportunities, among others, related to the implementation of sustainable business practices.

According to 2014 SME surveys in Armenia and Moldova (OECD, 2015a; 2015b), only 12% and 23.5% of the companies that undertake resource efficiency measures in the respective countries receive some technical or financial support (Figure 2.4). The larger the enterprise, the more likely it is to receive some support, which almost never reaches micro-businesses. The lack of government support appears to represent the biggest gap, in stark contrast with the extent of public support activities in the EU (EC, 2013).

Figure 2.4. **Percentage of SMEs receiving support for resource efficiency actions**

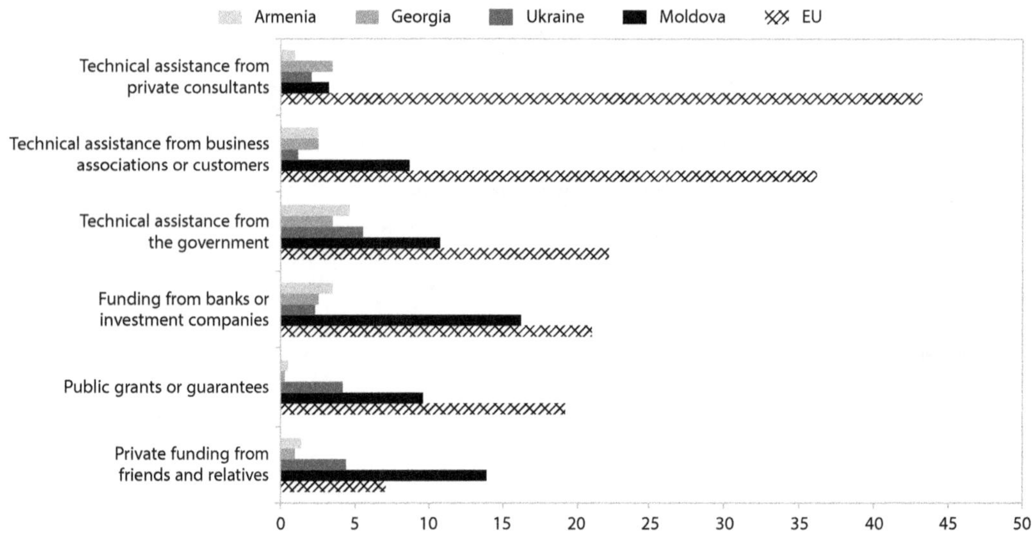

Sources: OECD (2016a), *Promoting better environmental performance of small and medium-sized enterprises in Ukraine*, www.oecd.org/env/outreach/Ukraine%20pilot%20project%20report%20EN.pdf; OECD (2016b), *Promoting better environmental performance of small and medium-sized enterprises in Georgia*, www.oecd.org/env/outreach/Georgia%20pilot%20project%20report%20final%20EN.pdf; OECD (2015a), *Promoting better environmental performance of small and medium-sized enterprises in Armenia*, www.oecd.org/environment/outreach/SME-greening-country-pilot-report-Armenia-en.pdf; OECD (2015b), *Promoting better environmental performance of small and medium-sized enterprises in Moldova*, www.oecd.org/environment/outreach/Binder%20English.pdf.

The positive role of the private sector also manifests itself through greening the supply chain initiatives. Azerbaijan is a good example of how larger companies can assist smaller companies to improve their environmental performance. In 2007, the Enterprise Development and Training Programme (EDTP) was launched with funding from British

Petroleum (BP) and its co-ventures. EDTP helps companies to develop their business and become a more competitive and environmentally friendly supplier to BP, its partners and the oil and gas industry as a whole.

Institutional challenges

The principal institutional barriers to enhancing green SME policies in the EaP region include the lack of capacity in environmental authorities to develop and implement sector-specific policies, the neglect of environmental compliance promotion activities, the weakness of the "green" component of SME support policies and institutions, and the shortage of resources (besides the limited donor funding) for the support of green business practices constitute.

Environmental authorities in EaP countries do not have specialised units in charge of promoting environmental compliance. Inspectorates are generally not responsible for compliance promotion activities. These functions are sometimes performed by an information centre within the environment ministry, which elaborates and disseminates environmental literature, educational guides, newsletters, digests and other informational materials.

Ministries of economy are the leading actors in the region working with SMEs. In several EaP countries, specialised SME support organisations have been established under the auspices of these ministries. The SME Development National Center of Armenia (SME DNC) was created in 2002 to provide state support to SMEs as well as to implement projects on SME sector development using state budgetary resources as well as contributions from international donor organisations. The SME DNC has a well-developed network of regional branches and representative offices covering all regions of Armenia and is co-ordinated by the central office in Yerevan. The SME DNC provides businesses with information, consulting services and training sessions. It also runs export promotion programmes, supports innovation and effective business models as well as administers financial loan guarantees to start-ups and operating businesses. However, it is only starting to develop activities to promote resource efficiency among SMEs.

In Moldova, the Organisation for Small and Medium Enterprises Sector Development (ODIMM) was created in 2007 as a special office with the main objective of fostering sustainable development of the SME sector. Enterprise Georgia was established in 2014 with a similar mandate.

Local governments can also stimulate SMEs to improve their environmental performance. Thanks to their local knowledge, they are often better placed than central governments to offer tailored measures for local SME development. However, due to financial constraints and other priorities, local governments of EaP countries are not always in a position to use this potential to the fullest. In Armenia and Moldova, local governments have statutory responsibilities in the field of environmental protection and the use of natural resources, but they are not implementing any specific programmes focused on improving SME environmental performance and compliance.

Another major institutional challenge in the region is the weakness of business associations. The existing business organisations, such as chambers of commerce and industry and employers' associations, are dominated by larger companies, do not give priority to serving the needs of small businesses, and have little knowledge of sustainable production issues. There are very few sector-specific trade associations (especially compared with their abundance in most OECD countries), and their SME membership is quite limited. Small businesses do not see the benefit of collaborating with their competitors and do not receive enough practical support from business associations in exchange for membership fees that they are asked to pay. This makes it much harder for the government to reach out to individual SMEs.

Conclusion

Although governments in EaP countries increasingly realise the importance of greening SMEs, and have introduced environmental considerations into their strategic documents on SME support activities, they have not yet introduced significant policy measures. Environmental regulatory regimes (such as permitting and inspections) are only starting to be more flexible based on the enterprises' level of environmental risk, still leaving a heavy administrative burden for SMEs. Environment ministries and their associate institutions provide regulatory information to businesses, but these information services rarely reach SMEs.

Governments in EaP countries generally play a passive role in promoting environmental sustainability and best practices among SMEs, and their involvement is generally limited to hosting international donor-funded projects. The lack of technical and financial government support for resource efficiency measures represents an important policy gap in promoting green practices.

References

EC (2013), *SMEs, Resource Efficiency and Green Markets*, Flash Eurobarometer 381, conducted by TNS Political & Social at the request of Directorate-General Enterprise and Industry, European Commission, Brussels, https://data.europa.eu/euodp/data/dataset/S1086_381.

OECD (2016a), *Promoting better environmental performance of small and medium-sized enterprises in Ukraine*, Pilot project report, Organisation for Economic Co-operation and Development, Paris, www.oecd.org/env/outreach/Ukraine%20pilot%20project%20report%20EN.pdf.

OECD (2016b), *Promoting better environmental performance of small and medium-sized enterprises in Georgia*, Pilot project report, Organisation for Economic Co-operation and Development, Paris, www.oecd.org/env/outreach/Georgia%20pilot%20project%20report%20final%20EN.pdf.

OECD (2015a), *Promoting better environmental performance of small and medium-sized enterprises in Armenia*, Pilot project report, Greening Economies in the Eastern Neighbourhood programme, Organisation for Economic Co-operation and Development, Paris, www.oecd.org/environment/outreach/SME-greening-country-pilot-report-Armenia-en.pdf.

OECD (2015b), *Promoting better environmental performance of small and medium-sized enterprises in Moldova*, Pilot project report, Greening Economies in the Eastern Neighbourhood programme, Organisation for Economic Co-operation and Development, Paris, www.oecd.org/environment/outreach/Binder%20English.pdf.

OECD (2007), *Small Businesses and Environmental Compliance: Review and Possible Application of International Experience in Georgia*, Organisation for Economic Co-operation and Development, Paris, https://www.oecd.org/countries/georgia/42072908.pdf.

Chapter 3

Environmental regulatory tools in OECD and EaP countries

This chapter looks at developments in environmental regulatory tools and how different approaches can more effectively support compliance. It begins with an exploration of changing trends in many OECD countries around simplifying environmental regulatory requirements for SMEs. These countries are doing so by replacing bespoke environmental permitting with standardised requirements (e.g. general binding rules) for specific activities with low environmental risk, provided that they involve a large number of operators and employ similar technologies. The chapter also looks at reducing the administrative burden on SMEs through collaboration between environmental and non-environmental regulators on identifying opportunities to reduce duplication in paperwork and conduct joint or delegated inspections in selected sectors. The increased effectiveness of a sector-based approach is also explored in the chapter, as part of a broader customer service perspective on the relationship between environmental regulators and SMEs.

Introduction

How environmental regulators approach low and high risk facilities can make a vital difference in allocating resources to support environmental compliance. Usually, environmental regulators do not have strategies that apply only to low-risk facilities – they simply have fewer resources to spend on them than on high-risk sites. However, an increasing number of environmental regulators in OECD countries are establishing special regimes for low-risk installations, the vast majority of which are SMEs.

Though permitting remains the dominant approach to regulating in most OECD countries, there has been a rapid expansion of standard rules – from simplified permitting to activity-based requirements without mandatory notification of the regulator – impacting a large number of SME sectors. Smaller businesses, often with limited in-house regulatory capacity, benefit from a standardised, rules-based approach to setting environmental requirements. It provides more certainty about the most effective way to achieve compliance than do individual, bespoke permits. Rule-based regimes also have other benefits, including reduced bureaucracy and costs to the regulator and the absence of impact on the level playing field within an industrial sector.

Shifting approaches to environmental regulation of SMEs in OECD countries

The trend to simplify regulatory requirements for SMEs is well illustrated by the introduction in 2009 in France of a new environmental regulatory regime – registration – for installations that present risk significant enough to justify its prior evaluation but that can be addressed through standardised regulatory requirements.[1] By the end of 2014, 35% of installations previously covered by permitting requirements were planned to be transferred to the registration regime. This is done for specific activity sectors (e.g. warehouses, petrol stations, drycleaners, small distilleries), activity volume thresholds being applied where necessary. The introduction of this new regime was the result of a gap between the administrative formality of a declaration and the extremely rigorous process of authorisation (permitting). The registration still requires the submission of an application and a simplified public consultation, but it has increased the predictability of the requirements and reduced the application processing time.

Another example of simplified permits is found in England and Wales, where local authorities issue air pollution permits to small businesses. The Department of Environment, Food and Rural Affairs (Defra) produces guidance notes for each of the 80 sectors regulated by local authorities. Developed by technical working groups in collaboration with business organisations, these guidance notes contain the descriptions of relevant best available techniques and emission limit values. In order to maintain a level playing field between local authorities across the country they are generally quite prescriptive.

Regulatory regimes for setting environmental requirements are usually organised in tiers based on the level of a facility's risk. In Scotland, SMEs that are not subject to integrated permitting can be regulated by simple licences/permits (with template conditions), a registration regime (involving a notification with information on who is engaging in relevant activities), or general binding rules (GBRs) where lower-risk activities (e.g. discharge into a surface water drainage system, storage and application of manure and fertilisers, etc.) do not require notification of the environmental regulator.

While the simplified permitting procedure always involves a formal application from the operator, which is approved by the regulatory authority at the sub-national or local level (although agencies in many countries increasingly use straightforward online application forms tailored to individual sectors), rules-based regimes may or may not require notification of, or registration with, the competent authority. ***Rules that require operators to notify, or register with, the competent environmental authority before engaging in an activity are preferable*** in terms of the regulator's knowledge of the regulated community and control over its potential environmental impacts.

Box 3.1. **General binding rules in the Netherlands**

In the Netherlands, there are different requirements for three categories of installations (defined in a 2008 government decree):

- Type A facilities, characterised by minimal environmental impact, are regulated by general, not activity-specific provisions; they do not need to notify the competent authority of their operations
- Type B installations have a moderate environmental impact, are covered by activity-specific GBRs and are required to notify the competent (local or provincial) authority of the nature and size of its activities four weeks before starting operations
- Type C installations have a potentially important impact and require an environmental licence which they have to comply with along with applicable activity-specific GBRs (this category includes large installations which are subject to the EU Industrial Emissions Directive and need an integrated permit/licence).

GBRs establish "quantitative target-based provisions" (i.e. emission limit values) that can be achieved by any "recognised" measure without prior consent from the competent authority as well as "qualitative" provisions that require certain specific techniques or management practices that can be modified only with the competent authority's consent.

GBRs have been developed for activities related to hazardous substances, plastics, metals, paper and textiles, food products, vehicles and other motorised equipment, etc. The range of activities subject to GBRs is expanding every year until 2016.

Source : Ministry of Infrastructure and the Environment, responses to the OECD questionnaire, January 2012.

There is no standard terminology to describe rules-based regulatory regimes across OECD countries. Terms such as "registration" and "general binding rules" mean different things in different systems. For example, in some countries (see Box 3.1, Type B installations for an example in the Netherlands) GBRs are defined as standard conditions specific to a type of activity or a sector with obligatory notification of environmental authorities before engaging in an activity. However, in others (e.g. in the UK) GBRs do not impose such a requirement. In the latter case, the system is similar to that of exemption from permitting, where the regulator does not know who is engaging in an activity to which the rules apply and how much low-risk activity is being conducted overall.

The following principal criteria should be applied when the use of GBRs or other rules-based regimes is considered for a segment of the regulated community:

- Rules must cover a sufficiently large number of regulated entities in a particular sector to make this regulatory regime effective.
- The state of technology and techniques in that sector must not be fast moving, as rules cannot be updated frequently.
- The facilities must have a similar, low-risk environmental impact.

Even a GBR regime with mandatory notification does not always give enough information to the regulator. Installations under the "declaration" regime in France are subject to GBRs that are laid out in standardised ministerial orders (*arrêtés-types*). These requirements are attached to the formal acknowledgement of receipt of a declaration which is sent by the prefect to the operator. In some cases, they may be made more stringent by an order of the prefect to reflect local conditions. However, the inspection services do not usually have an opportunity to review a declaration or recommend rejecting it. There is a consequent problem of the lack of knowledge of low-risk SMEs by environmental regulatory authorities.

The notification issue can be addressed by requiring operators to regularly assess their own compliance with the rules and submit a respective statement to the competent environmental authority. For example, the Small Quantity Hazardous Waste Generator Education and Self-Certification Program in the US state of New Hampshire (in place since 2003) requires the state's approximately 3 700 enterprises to conduct a facility assessment every three years and provide a declaration to the New Hampshire Department of Environmental Services that the company is in compliance with the applicable rules.

The pilot project on SME greening in Ukraine produced guidance on simplified environmental regulation for SMEs. This guidance (Chapter 9) presents several simplified regulatory regimes suitable for installations with low environmental impact, including GBRs and registration. It also identifies appropriate economic sectors for simplified environmental regulation and analyses the implications of their introduction in Ukraine.

Better regulation initiatives for small businesses

Small businesses often complain that keeping up to date with environmental requirements is burdensome, particularly in relation to understanding which requirements apply in their individual context. Finding guidance and advice explaining what they have to do to comply with given regulations is difficult. SMEs often feel that they are not supported enough and are unreasonably expected to cope with the same levels of paperwork and obligations as larger companies. Businesses generally express support for a customer-focused relationship between regulators and the regulated with the primary goal of compliance rather than enforcement. Improved information for regulated entities has been consistently identified as the most important factor for reducing the administrative burden on businesses (EA, 2011).

A recent UK survey (Defra, 2011b) suggests that micro-businesses spend more time on activities associated with demonstrating compliance (preparing for inspections, completing paperwork, record-keeping) than actual activities to comply with regulations. Despite efforts to reduce unnecessary duplication of inspections, business are still often required to provide the same information more than once in demonstrating compliance with regulations.

Similarly, the first of the UK Government's five principles of better regulation[2] is the proportionality of regulation, which presumes regulating small businesses only where necessary and with practical exemptions. For rules that will have a significant impact on small businesses, soliciting their input at the drafting stage reduces eventual adverse effects. The US Small Business Regulatory Enforcement Fairness Act (1996) provides SMEs with an expanded opportunity to participate in the development of certain regulations. Some European countries require regulatory agencies to prepare special statements on the potential impact of proposed regulations on small businesses.

Listing the full range of regulations that have an impact on small businesses in selected sectors helps to identify opportunities to reduce duplication in paperwork and/or processes among regulatory authorities. Among different ways to simplify the administrative requirements for reporting on environmental issues and avoid duplication of requested information are the creation of nationwide information registration systems accessible by all competent government authorities, the introduction of e-government to replace paperwork documentation, and the implementation of the "one-window" approach for issuing appropriate permits and licences to businesses (e.g. through local authorities). Offering compliance-related information to businesses (Chapter 4) also contributes to better regulation by reducing their transaction cost of compliance.

Incentives for environmental management certification

While the main driver for businesses to have a certified environmental management system (EMS) is market demand from customers and clients (the adaptation of EMSs to the specifics of small businesses is addressed in Chapter 4), environmental authorities may offer additional regulatory incentives:

- The adoption of an ISO 14 001 EMS or a similar standard may entitle operators to certain ***privileges in the permitting process***. In the Netherlands, EMS-certified operators can apply for licences that are less detailed and prescriptive. Several EU countries (e.g. Italy, Slovakia) issue permits with longer validity periods and with reduced reporting requirements to EMAS-certified companies (EC, 2004b).
- The US EPA's Small Business Compliance Policy allows small businesses to obtain ***reductions in monetary penalties*** if violations are discovered by any voluntary means, including government-sponsored on-site compliance assistance activities or environmental audits,[3] EMSs, use of online compliance assistance tools, etc. In Austria, administrative fines are waived for businesses with a certified EMS if they detect non-compliance during an internal audit.
- ***The inspection frequency*** may also be directly or indirectly linked to the presence and quality of the operator's EMS. Companies with a certified EMS enjoy reduced inspection frequency in Norway, and in France installations registered with EMAS (there were only 17 such installations in April 2011) are exempted from routine compliance inspections. In Korea, "green companies" designated by the Ministry of Environment are exempted from routine environmental reporting, and their inspection frequency is reduced.

Still, while there is some reliance on EMSs to facilitate compliance, the experience of many regulators (e.g. in the UK and the US) is that an EMS is far from being a guarantee of compliance (especially since ISO 14 001 does not account for compliance). Therefore, there may not be sufficient reason for special treatment of EMS-certified businesses in compliance monitoring.

Sectoral approach to compliance assurance

Regulatory requirements (such as GBRs) are usually driven by the type of environmental impact, although they tend to affect specific sectors. However, compliance assurance in general and particularly compliance promotion are predominantly sector-based. Small businesses typically respond only to messages adapted to their activity sector (discussed further in Chapter 4) which makes the sectoral approach crucial in promoting compliance and green practices among SMEs.

A growing number of environmental enforcement authorities produce sectoral strategies that seek to optimise the balance between the three pillars of compliance assurance – compliance promotion, monitoring/assessment and enforcement – in relation to the needs and challenges of a specific segment of the regulated community. As a result, a significant share of compliance monitoring/assessment activities is becoming sector-based, although it continues to rely on impact-based regulations.

In many sectors, themed and special inspections (inspection campaigns) have been increasingly used to monitor low-risk sites or activities. ***Rotating sector-specific campaigns could be a strategy for maximising the impact of limited agency resources.*** Such campaigns can create the impression of a substantial regulatory capability and threat of enforcement, with a very limited regulatory resource commitment. It is advisable to ***link awareness campaigns and inspection campaigns***: the former give businesses information to comply while the latter, after a certain period, seek to establish a level playing field through compliance monitoring and enforcement. However, inspectors taking part in such an inspection campaign should not focus exclusively on thematic risks but also pay attention to site-specific risks and requirements.

Reliance on complaints and reports from the public remains a necessary and even, given the resource constraints, inevitable part of compliance monitoring of SMEs. However, while complaints have the potential to uncover new risks and risk-posing businesses, they are often driven by immediate concerns that may not be related to the regulators priorities or even fall under its mandate, thus dissipating agency resources.

In order to optimise compliance monitoring of non-complex, low-risk installations, it is advisable for environmental enforcement authorities to co-operate with non-environmental regulators and private sector organisations in their inspection activities. For example, Scotland's Environmental and Rural Services (SEARS) partnership of eight Scottish regulators with competencies over the farming and forestry sectors ensures co-ordinated inspections and streamlined reporting procedures. SEARS partners arrange joint visits or entrust one or two of the partners to inspect the aspects that are normally under the other organisations' jurisdiction. They also share information provided by the farmers and other relevant businesses, thereby reducing the administrative burden on the regulated community, and co-ordinate the handling of customer enquiries. The Scottish Environment Protection Agency (SEPA), the environmental regulator, trains staff of other partner agencies that conduct regular site visits according to their own mandates but also perform certain environmental regulatory responsibilities delegated by SEPA.

Outsourcing of compliance monitoring to non-government bodies may be more appropriate at the local level, where competent authorities often lack capacity to properly exercise this function. In Ireland, Dublin City Council has appointed a contractor to implement its Fats, Oils and Grease programme to reduce grease discharges from food service establishments (pubs, restaurants, hotels, etc.), thereby preventing blockages in the public drainage network. The contractor's role is to identify premises that require an effluent licence, to advise the operator on best management practices, and to inspect the premises four times a year to ensure compliance with licence conditions. In putting in place such an arrangement, the competent governmental authority should set clear requirements for the contractor's performance and review it periodically.

Conclusion

Across the OECD, countries are moving to simplify environmental regulatory requirements for SMEs. Most commonly, this is being done by a shift from permitting requirements to rules-based regimes aimed at specific activity sectors and for specific thresholds. There are substantive differences among countries in terms of how GBRs are defined and implemented, including whether they are administered through national, sub-national or local government, how and when notification is required, and how facilities are defined. Although GBRs are usually environmental impact-driven rather than sector driven, taking a sectoral approach to compliance assurance and information helps ensure success. Simplified EMS systems can help SMEs with better environmental practices, but they are not guarantors of environmental compliance. Ultimately, implementing better regulation that reduces the burden on both SMEs and regulators depends not just on the regime but on co-ordination among regulatory bodies, and consultation with industry groups.

Notes

1. In this case, the term "registration" refers to a simplified permitting regime.
2. PACTT principles of better regulation: proportionate, accountable, consistent, targeted and transparent (BRE, 2010).
3. The EPA Audit Policy prescribes, among others, an audit protocol which summarises key statutory requirements and contains a regulatory checklist with detailed procedures for conducting an audit of facility operations.

References

Defra (2011a), *Business Perspectives on Approaches to Securing Compliance*, Greenstreet Berman Ltd. report for Defra and Environment Agency, Department for Environment, Food and Rural Affairs, http://randd.defra.gov.uk/Document.aspx?Document=CL2463EADefraBusinessapproachestocomplianceR2V6FCA.pdf.

Defra (2011b), *Micro businesses and environmental regulation*, Final Report prepared by GHK Consulting Ltd. for Defra, Department for Environment, Food and Rural Affairs, http://randd.defra.gov.uk/Document.aspx?Document=Deframicrobusiness_FINALREPORT.pdf.

EA (2011), *Effectiveness of Regulation: Literature Review and Analysis*, Report SC090028, Environment Agency, Bristol, UK, https://www.gov.uk/government/uploads/system/uploads/attachment_data/file/290502/scho0911bubh-e-e.pdf.

EA (2009), *Understanding and Improving SME Compliance*, Report SC080017/R2, Resource efficiency programme, Evidence Directorate, Environment Agency, Bristol, UK, https://www.gov.uk/government/uploads/system/uploads/attachment_data/file/291208/scho1209brpv-e-e.pdf.

EC (2007), *Small, clean and competitive: A programme to help small and medium-sized enterprises comply with environmental legislation*, Case studies and good practices in environmental compliance assistance, Commission staff working document, European Commission, Brussels, 8.10.2007, ec.europa.eu/environment/archives/sme/pdf/exec_summary_en.pdf.

EC (2004), Annex to the *Report from the Commission to the Council and the European Parliament on Incentives for EMAS Registered Organisations*, Commission Staff Working Document, European Commission, Brussels, http://ec.europa.eu/transparency/regdoc/rep/1/2004/EN/1-2004-745-EN-F1-1.Pdf.

Chapter 4

Information-based instruments and improved messaging around SMEs' environmental requirements

This chapter looks at how the type of information and the way it is conveyed can support environmental compliance by SMEs and encourage green business practices. Packaging the information and formulating the right message is crucial for the effectiveness of communication tools. Small businesses have particular needs, with significant heterogeneity across and even within sectors. Information-based instruments are more effective when messages are tailored to the nature and needs of small businesses. Explaining the economic benefits for SMEs of improved environmental performance is an important component of environmental outreach.

In this chapter, the experiences of different OECD countries and EaP countries are documented. The role of environmental management systems (EMSs) with varying degrees of complexity and lower administrative burdens, as well as sectoral green label schemes, are discussed in terms of their attractiveness to small businesses, in contrast to formal ISO 14001 certification. Sector-specific green certification (of business practices) and eco-label schemes (for products) also contribute to an increased demand for green business practices.

Introduction

SMEs, particularly micro-businesses, often do not have substantive resource or expertise devoted to environmental compliance. The same regulatory approaches that might work for large companies may be challenging for SMEs to interpret and respond to. Businesses are told that they have a duty to act in an environmentally responsible way, but it is often unclear what this actually means, how a business can do it and at what cost. Going beyond compliance represents an even bigger challenge, where the lack of awareness of cost-effective opportunities is the key bottleneck.

Governments, in collaboration with business groups, can address these challenges by providing SMEs with information on green practices. Among information dissemination tools, one can distinguish between advice and guidance. Advice is active, direct engagement with a business face-to-face during inspection visits or audits, answering telephone, e-mail or website help requests, as well as addressing business representatives at seminars and similar events. Guidance is the provision of information to regulated entities, typically in the written (printed or electronic) form. Guidance includes, among others, e-mail updates, website free-access guidance pages, leaflets, brochures and other publications.

Designing effective messages

The majority of European SMEs act to become more resource-efficient in order to reduce costs (63%), while 23% are driven by the customer demand. The growing number of SMEs taking resource efficiency actions says that their production costs have decreased as a result: 42% in 2013 compared to 35% just a year earlier. More than two-thirds of SMEs are satisfied with the return on their investments in resource efficiency (EC, 2013).

In addition to financial benefits (Table 4.1), implementing green practices may result in commercial benefits (new business opportunities, preferred supplier status, etc.), organisational benefits (derived from improvements in the quality of management), communication benefits (positive public image, better relationships with customers, investors and regulators), and increased employee motivation and morale. These benefits are confirmed by small businesses

Table 4.1. **Cost savings from environmental improvements in SMEs**

Areas of improvement	Sources of savings
Process efficiency	Optimising the performance of existing processes (or introducing more efficient new ones) minimises the use of raw materials, energy and water and the production of waste. Proper maintenance of equipment minimises costly downtime and resource waste associated with shutdown and start-up periods.
Product design	It may be possible to re-design a product so as to reduce the amount of resources it contains while still maintaining the level of service it provides.
Waste disposal	Improving process efficiency reduces the amount of waste that a process produces. Once waste has been generated, it is often possible to reuse it or pass it on to other companies that can use it, and thus avoid the costs of its disposal.
Source of raw materials	Changing the source of raw materials in a particular process by switching to recycled materials can result in cost savings.
Infrastructure	It is possible to generate savings by making efficiency changes in the company's infrastructure: installing energy-efficient lighting, insulating buildings, improving the efficiency of heating systems.
Packaging and transport	The reduction of packaging volume and finding local suppliers and customers to decrease transportation distances can be major sources of cost savings.

Source: Starkey, 1998, *Environmental Management Tools for SMEs: A Handbook.*

themselves: Scottish SMEs named reduced operating costs, a more motivated workforce, reduced risk of prosecution or fines, and improved customer relationships as key business gains from improving their environmental performance (NetRegs, 2009).

For micro-businesses, improved local image, increased number of customers and staff morale appear to be the main incentives for better environmental practices (Defra, 2011b). At the same time, most small businesses are concerned that improved image or increased sales are unlikely to result from compliance with environmental requirements because customers are not aware of a business's operational practices and, therefore, this does not influence their customer choice.

Despite numerous empirical studies which have demonstrated that improving the environmental performance of a firm also improves its financial performance, many SMEs are concerned about the short term costs of enhancing their environmental performance, and there is an inherent conflict between protecting the environment and the need to keep down costs and run a successful business. The challenge is to ***convince SMEs that green practices actually reduce costs and make for better business***.

Since by far the biggest concern of SMEs is short-term financial profitability, the fact that environmental management can save money, reduce costs and increase efficiency is usually well received by business owners. Thus, regardless of whether the objective is to improve compliance, influence the uptake of environmental technologies or increase the adoption of EMSs, environmental information targeting small businesses should make the "business case" and illustrate the financial benefits of environmental improvements.

Most small businesses seek clear and consistent information on the minimum requirements for compliance. Interpretation of text-heavy guidance can be difficult for an SME. ***There should be a simple message about the problem, its solution (step-by-step guidance) and where to go for more information***. The most efficient way of providing advice and guidance to businesses is to take into account the full suite of regulations that apply to them, not just environmental regulations. Regulatory requirements that are communicated to small businesses should be well co-ordinated across government.

To avoid excessive or unnecessary costs for businesses, ***guidance should clearly state the minimum legal requirements***. As the volume and complexity of both mandatory and voluntary (good practice) guidance grow, businesses are concerned that it is becoming more difficult to differentiate between the two and that voluntary guidance can sometimes be treated as mandatory in practice. Misleading advice could lead to over-compliance and an unnecessary increase in the regulatory burden. To avoid this, ***compliance and good practice guidance should be clearly distinguished***.

Businesses like compliance guidance to be legally defensible (exonerating them of potential sanctions if the guidance is accurately followed). Poor guidance which is not adapted to the needs of small businesses leaves business owners worrying that they are doing something wrong and that when they try to do the right thing, they can be penalised for not getting it absolutely right. On the other hand, too much advice and guidance may restrict innovation in finding solutions that are cost-effective for the operator's specific circumstances, potentially putting smaller businesses at a competitive disadvantage.

It is crucial to emphasise that what is good in environmental terms may also be good for the financial bottom line. For example, the best practices guide for garages produced by the Irish EPA's National Waste Prevention Programme is called "Smart Garage Guide: Save money and improve the performance of your garage". Using the same approach, the EPA's Green Business Initiative (www.greenbusiness.ie), launched in 2006, seeks primarily to enable businesses to use web-based audit/assessment tools to assess their own resource use efficiency, particularly with respect to waste and water. The Green Business web pages also offer tips and case studies on how to save money by reducing resource use.

In making the "business case", it may be particularly useful to present examples of other similar companies receiving commercial benefits as a result of the environmental management improvements in question. Case studies should preferably be local in order to increase the acceptance of their conclusions by small businesses. However, the experience shows that case studies lose their importance as the promotion programme matures.

How such information is packaged, what message it presents, and how and who delivers it, is critically important to its positive impact. The key sector-specific factors affecting the choice and implementation of promotional tools include the following:

- the degree of uniformity in size and management practices of the industry – the greater the diversity, the greater the need to develop different strategies and instruments for different sub-categories of businesses
- the level of technological sophistication in the industry, which may determine the need for detailed guidance
- the existence of a well-organised industry association representing the sector, which affects the mode of communication with individual businesses
- the public profile of the industry, which may determine the extent to which SMEs may be susceptible to public pressure.

The most appropriate communication channels are likely to be sector-specific, reflecting the different business models and activities within different sectors. Public authorities tend to be best suited to delivering "one-way" information, whereas hands-on support is better delivered by business associations or private organisations (the institutional aspects are further discussed in Chapter 6). When guidance comes from a private sector organisation, it is generally perceived by small businesses as reliable, while information received from governmental bodies is often regarded with suspicion. At the same time, encouraging as many businesses as possible across all sectors to access centrally available web-based resources can contribute to the cost-effective, consistent delivery of regulatory guidance.

To make sure the information directed at SMEs is relevant, ***working with industry in formulating sector-specific guidance and codes of practice is of primary importance***. Giving businesses a say in the structure and content of environmental guidance increases the likelihood that the material is understandable and resonates with business owners. The extent to which SMEs are willing to participate in the design of information tools and other incentives largely depends on the existence of established business organisations.

It may be difficult to persuade SMEs to act upon environmental information, even when it is obviously in their own financial interest. Information generally has an impact on companies which already have an environmental interest, but may struggle to reach those who are not already interested in green practices. Evidence from the literature suggests that raising business awareness by providing them with more information on their environmental impact will not automatically lead to changes in behaviour (Defra, 2011b). Other considerations are at least as critical, primarily the need to strengthen market incentives for environmental improvements by directly (supply chain pressure, green public procurement) and indirectly (green certifications and eco-labels) increasing the demand for environmentally friendly products and services.

Proactive information dissemination

The simplest tool to disseminate regulatory information is a "***regulatory watch***" – a (paid or free) subscription service sending regular e-mail or mobile phone updates on relevant legislative developments and new applicable regulatory requirements. One example of such a service, usually established by trade or business support organisations, is *Enviroveille* in France, managed by the Assembly of French Chambers of Commerce and Industry.

Several environmental authorities organise ***help desks*** to respond to compliance questions from businesses and other stakeholders. The Swedish EPA operates a so-called "legal support service" available by telephone for two hours every working day, which offers advice and interpretation on legal issues. The US EPA's Asbestos and Small Business Ombudsman answers technical and regulatory questions coming from small businesses on a toll-free hotline, in addition to developing other compliance assistance tools. Some agencies in OECD countries are exploring the possibility of tapping into social networks to provide compliance assistance.

Many regulators find providing ***direct compliance assistance to operators during inspection visits*** to be an effective strategy for dealing with particular types of regulated entities, particularly SMEs that are generally willing to comply but who are not aware of the regulatory requirements or who lack the organisational capacity to comply (SNIFFER, 2011). The aim is for operators to see the regulator as not only a "good policeman" but as a "good advisor" and to save on costs of working out what they are supposed to do and how. Such "advise and assist" visits can be formally distinguished from compliance inspections in an enforcement agency's plan of activities. In Finland, inspectors have regular discussions with operators on existing and potential compliance problems and possible solutions; and the results of such discussions are recorded in the electronic compliance monitoring system (OECD, 2009). However, this instrument has an associated risk of "capture", as inspectors may start to see the world through the eyes of the firms they are advising. Such advisory visits are also quite resource-intensive.

Industry magazines, newsletters and business or community events are seen to be helpful methods of advertising regulatory requirements and enforcement cases,[1] particularly to some small or rural businesses which may not have access to the internet. ***Workshops, training seminars and industry fairs*** (particularly those organised by trade organisations and other business groups) can also be effective in conveying information or generic advice on how to comply with the requirements. They can facilitate positive relations between regulators and regulated businesses, help share good practices and foster co-operative approaches to addressing environmental issues.

Non-governmental organisations such as Cleaner Production Centres can also provide information on green practices, targeted at specific audiences – industry as well as national and local governments. Other tools that the Centres can use include seminars, workshops and conferences focusing on information dissemination and exchange. However, it may be difficult to attract SME operators to attend such sessions, as they usually do not have dedicated environmental personnel. In addition, these events are not necessarily helpful in seeking meaningful feedback on the content of environmental guidance.

On the other hand, ***targeted, concise, user-friendly guides*** can be very useful in delivering a message that adhering to environmentally friendly practices (and thereby complying with the law) is a smart way to do business. ***Such guides should illustrate the "business benefits first" approach to promoting good environmental behaviour.***

The dissemination of compliance assistance information to the regulated community is best achieved in partnership with multiple stakeholders. For example, the pocket-size "Small Environmental Guide for Construction Workers" prepared jointly by the Scottish EPA and the Construction Industry Research and Information Association targets professional contractors working on all types of construction sites. It advocates that "working in an 'environmentally friendly' way can help to improve business performance and save you money in the process. "Getting it right ... helps you to stay in business". There are also examples of cross-sectoral guides for SMEs, including the "Environment and Energy Guide for SMEs" issued by the Assembly of French Chambers of Commerce and Industry (ACFCI, 2010).

Web-based guidance tools

The key feature of comprehensive information-based assistance programmes is that enterprises can get advice, informational and methodological materials in one place. Over the last decade, in many OECD countries there has been rapid proliferation of ***government-sponsored business advisory websites, especially targeting SMEs***. Government authorities like online guidance tools because they offer regulatory consistency of advice, time and cost savings on face-to-face advice as well as anonymity which facilitates communication with the regulated community.

Environmental guidance can be delivered through environmental regulators' own websites, specialised sites funded by governmental authorities (those could also be ministries of economies, industry or agriculture) and generic business portals which direct users to information on environmental compliance and good practices. However, the development and operation of such programmes require significant funding.

The US EPA's online National Compliance Assistance Centers (www.assistancecenters.net, created in 1998) deliver information through websites for 16 manufacturing and services sectors, federal facilities and local governments. The EPA also runs a Small Business Gateway (www.epa.gov/smallbusiness) which, among others, provides information on environmental assistance and technical help available from the Agency. In addition, the US Small Business Environmental Home Page (www.smallbiz-enviroweb.org) is intended to be a "one-stop shop" for small businesses and assistance providers who seek information on a wide range of environmental topics. It directs users to compliance information (including links to state websites), fact sheets on environmental best management practices in ten SME sectors (bakeries, service stations, retail stores, etc.), key small business publications, information on upcoming events, etc.

NetRegs (Box 4.1), a web-based tool created in partnership between the UK environmental regulators (for England and Wales, Scotland, and Northern Ireland), provided between 2002 and 2011 free environmental guidance to small and medium-sized businesses throughout the country. Since 2012 this service has been run in Scotland and Northern Ireland only by the Scottish Environment Protection Agency (SEPA) and the Northern Ireland Environment Agency (NIEA). Sector guidelines are tailored to provide specific guidance on environmental legislation and as well as good practices applicable to the processes in each sector, while distinguishing between the mandatory and the voluntary. A library of environmental topics contains practical explanations of issues such as packaging, waste, clean air and effluent management which are relevant to all businesses regardless of their industry sector. The distinct customer service focus of the tool was developed in part through regular surveys of user businesses, supported by a Business Advisory Group comprising business representatives.

Box 4.1. NetRegs: An internet-based compliance assistance tool in the UK

NetRegs, launched in 2002, is a web-based tool created in partnership between the UK environmental regulators (for England and Wales, Scotland, and Northern Ireland), now running in Scotland and Northern Ireland only, provides free environmental guidance to small and medium-sized businesses. The content is developed jointly by the regulatory authorities but is customised for Scotland's and Northern Ireland's context. NetRegs includes:

- guidance by business type for 112 sectors in agriculture, construction, offices, etc.
- a searchable library of environmental topics
- guidance on existing and forthcoming national and EU legislation and a free e-update service, which provides regular updates on changes in the environmental legislation
- a self-assessment questionnaire that enabled businesses to discover more about what they must do to fully comply with environmental legislation
- interactive learning modules (e.g. on more complex pieces of legislation)
- video case studies illustrating good practice
- a postcode-driven "waste directory" containing a matrix of waste recycling and disposal contacts
- links to trade associations and other sources of environmental guidance and business support.

NetRegs undertakes biennial telephone surveys to understand how SMEs perceive their environmental performance and the assistance they get in improving it. In the last UK survey (2009), a total of 7 000 businesses were interviewed across the four UK countries and 10 business sectors. According to the survey, small businesses' reasons for using NetRegs were: to find out how to comply with the law (56.4%), to find all the relevant information in one place (23.4%), to build the business's green credentials (10.2%), and to find out how to reduce waste (7%).

NetRegs had over 470 000 unique monthly visitors in 2011, about 60% of which were SMEs (the rest being larger businesses, consulting firms, local authorities, etc.) It was estimated that by using the NetRegs service, UK SMEs were saving an estimated GBP 58 million annually, an average of GBP 2 600 per business. The project's start-up costs were GBP 3.5 million and the operating cost for the UK-wide service was about GBP 1 million per year (it is now GBP 250 000 per year).

Source : NetRegs (2011), www.netregs.org.uk.

As part of the UK Transformational Government Agenda, England's Environment Agency had to withdraw from the NetRegs partnership as well as move its own website to a single gov.uk portal. The idea was to facilitate user navigation to different types of business-related advice and to save government resources. However, much of the environmental content has been removed in the process.

Environmental assistance to European SMEs is also available from the European Commission (EC). An SME portal created on its DG Environment website (ec.europa.eu/environment/sme) provides access to relevant legislation, information, tools and available training. The Environmental Compliance Assistance Programme (ECAP) established in 2007 maintains a website which offers an online best practice database which helps businesses implement European environmental legislation and minimise the environmental impact of their activities. The EC also supports the recently created GreenEcoNet green practice information platform (Box 4.2).

Box 4.2. **GreenEcoNet: The first pan-European website for SME greening**

Launched in June 2014, GreenEcoNet is the first pan-European website aiming to connect SMEs and support them in finding green business solutions and tools as well as sources of finance. It displays real life case studies from SMEs across Europe that have successfully gone "green", profiles a library of tools and guidance, and supports discussion forums and news updates tailored for smaller businesses.

Funded by the European Commission, the website is part of a wider programme of workshops and networking opportunities co-ordinated by the GreenEcoNet consortium, including the Green Economy Coalition (London), Stockholm Environment Institute, Ecologic Institute (Berlin), Centre for European Policy Studies (Brussels), and others.

Source : GreenEcoNet (2015), www.greeneconet.eu.

Designing and launching an online guidance tool is not enough: ***there needs to be an effective communication strategy to ensure that businesses continue to use and benefit from it.*** Web-based tools should be supplemented by other instruments (such as mailings, brochures, workshops) which can add significant value. At the same time, while mail and face-to-face contact may continue to be an important route for outreach to small businesses in the short term, improving access to, and use of, the internet among small businesses is likely to be a more sustainable and cost-effective form of communication in the longer term.

Direct capacity building

A recent review of SME support initiatives on resource efficiency in EU member states (EC, 2014a) identified about 230 technical assistance programmes supporting businesses in the identification and implementation of resource efficiency measures. Over half of those programmes provide general access to information, self-assessment tools, case studies, etc. Others offer tailored, face-to-face services to individual companies. While general programmes also provide assistance with resource efficiency audits and setting up EMS schemes, these tend to operate mostly on one-to-many basis (for example, through workshops or training events) and address general approaches and methodologies rather than deal with individual companies.

The role of government authorities in providing technical assistance to businesses is not as extensive as in the implementation of other policy instruments. The practical implementation of these activities is mainly carried out by special business support organisations established by the government (Box 4.3). NGOs such as Cleaner Production Centres as well as consulting companies may also play this role, while the government may provide them with financial support.

Hands-on, direct resource efficiency support programmes seek to bridge the gap between providing general knowledge and applying it to specific circumstances of individual businesses by assisting companies to identify both opportunities and means for implementing resource efficiency measures, as well as their potential costs and benefits.

Non-government actors such as National Cleaner Production Centres can provide ***face-to-face advice to businesses through audits of different aspects of their environmental management***, demonstration projects and their follow-up. Capacity building and support for enterprises may also cover activities such as ***development and dissemination of methodological materials and case studies, as well as the implementation of training programmes.***

Box 4.3. Green Offer by Enterprise Ireland

Enterprise Ireland is the government organisation responsible for the development and growth of Irish enterprises in world markets, with particular emphasis on SMEs. In addition to efforts to enhance environmental awareness and improve performance in Irish industry through its environmental information portal, Envirocentre.ie, Enterprise Ireland's Green Offer aims to increase the adoption of green business principles by its clients. The Green Offer comprises three programmes:

- The Green Start programme helps SMEs, at no cost to them, to establish a simple environmental management system by conducting a site audit and providing advice on regulatory compliance issues, green market positioning, preparation of an environmental policy, etc.
- Green Plus is meant to build on Green Start and to assist companies to develop products and services to a level where they comply with specific green procurement requirements. This may involve the implementation of an accredited EMS, improvements in products or processes or applying for eco-labels.
- Finally, Green Transform is designed to further improve the competitiveness and market access of those companies who have maximised their energy efficiency or reduced their carbon footprint.

Source : Enterprise Ireland (2015), www.envirocentre.ie.

To ensure sustainable application of resource efficiency and other green practices, there is a need to educate company mangers. Long-term on-the-job training, combined with train-the-trainer courses, is the most effective way to build professional capacity among small businesses. Senior managers may be targeted through short sessions focusing on the basics of environmental management and its benefits and challenges, enabling them to motivate their staff. An overall aim of such training programmes should be to integrate environmental concerns into the mainstream business strategy.

An innovative way of advising small businesses has been developed by the Green Business Partnership (Scotland), whose popular Bright Green Placements programme has been organising for already over 15 years two-three month student placements in SMEs to follow up on environmental audits and work with the company's management to implement the recommended measures (and achieve related savings). A similar initiative was to offer an "ad hoc environmental manager" for one day per month to a small business that cannot afford a dedicated environmental manager in order to help it with environmental management activities.

The number of firms likely to engage in implementing good practices as a result of direct, hands-on capacity building activities, as well as the potential economic and environmental benefits that may arise from these programmes are likely to be influenced by the following factors:

- ***Involving multiple public sector organisations and industry associations*** in programme design, implementation and strategic oversight can provide a broader perspective and better co-ordinated support to SMEs. For example, the Danish Green Network is run jointly by public and private sector representatives. The regional *Performance Bretagne Environnement Plus* (PBE+) programme in France is funded jointly by the Regional Council, the central government, the local employers' union and the Chamber of Commerce and Industry.

- ***Affordability*** of the support services has a major influence on their uptake by SMEs. The services should be provided free of charge or at reduced fee rates (subsidised by grants, see Chapter 5).
- Programmes that provide ***long-term support*** allow fine-tuning of their services and have a longer-lasting impact.
- ***Consideration of economic impacts*** of green practices (on companies' profitability, employment, competitiveness, etc.) can be expected to increase the uptake of the programme.
- ***Promoting the programme's achievements***, including by publicising success as case studies, can encourage other companies to implement green practices.
- ***Using local delivery partners*** enables capacity building programmes to gain local knowledge, credibility and accountability.
- ***Regular, independent and impartial evaluation*** of the programme as a whole and the benefit to individual companies can lead to continual improvement.

Recognition of green practices

Simplified environmental management systems

A recent EU-wide study (Calogirou et al., 2010) has shown that despite government incentives (Chapter 3) only 0.4% of European SMEs have a formally certified EMS. According to a British survey (NetRegs, 2009), just under 4% of the SMEs surveyed stated that they had an EMS in place. Around a quarter of all businesses had an environmental policy, and the likelihood of this increased with the size of the business. Just about one-tenth of small businesses considered that an EMS would be "quite useful" or "very useful", and the fewer employees they had, the less favourably they viewed the benefits of such a system. Although supply chain pressure in some sectors is a powerful driver for some SMEs to adopt an EMS, small businesses face serious obstacles, including a lack of resources, knowledge and technical capacity, the fact that most EMS-related costs are upfront and benefits are medium-term, as well as low public visibility.

The challenge is to tailor EMSs, both in terms of their content and delivery, to the particularities of SMEs. The key, at least for smaller businesses, is to focus on simple, accessible improvements in management practices, rather than the introduction of a formal, administratively complex EMS.

There are initiatives in several OECD countries, mostly coming from the private sector, to design simplified EMSs suitable for small businesses. *Econcertive* is an Irish company which provides environmental support to businesses and organisations in all sectors, primarily by means of the EcoCert scheme (www.ecocert.ie). The requirements for achieving EcoCert certification are the same core requirements as for any recognised EMS standard, but the paperwork is minimal. In addition, the certification process includes the identification of energy, waste and water-related savings (with a money-back performance guarantee).

The Association of French Chambers of Commerce and Industry (ACFCI) leads two initiatives on "EMS-light", with substantial technical, methodological and financial assistance from the public Environment and Energy Management Agency (ADEME). The "1.2.3 Environment" programme is designed to facilitate step-by-step ISO 14001 certification. *EnVol* is a special environmental management programme for small businesses (with less than 50 employees) that do not aspire fully fledged ISO 14001 certification but would like to get recognition for their basic EMS, which roughly corresponds to the first level of "1.2.3 Environment" (ACFCI, 2010).

The "green tick" logo launched by Scotland's Green Business Partnership in February 2011 is another example of making corporate environmental management accessible to SMEs. One tick demonstrates that the company has an environmental policy, assessed its legal compliance and is committed to making continual environmental improvements. The accreditation with two ticks means that the business, in addition, manages its compliance and has an environmental action plan. Three ticks signify the existence of a fully-fledged environmental management system.

There are also examples of SME-focused national environmental certification programmes conducted with active involvement of local governments, such as the Eco-Lighthouse Programme in Norway (Box 4.4).

Box 4.4. **Environmental certification of SMEs in Norway**

The Eco-Lighthouse Programme is a programme for environmental certification of SMEs in Norway. With this programme, companies are supposed to reduce their impact on the environment, reduce costs and make use of an environmental profile in their marketing. The Programme is supported by the Norwegian Ministry of the Environment.

The Eco Lighthouse Office is responsible for marketing at the national level and the continuous development of the programme (including developing and improving trade demands in co-operation with consultants, companies and branch organisations). The office also arranges training courses for consultants who conduct environmental audits and local government staff responsible for certifying companies.

The municipalities recruit new companies, establish contacts between consultants and companies, make use of the media and carry out inspections before the environmental certificate is awarded. The municipalities also issue the certificates when the companies have implemented the action plan to satisfy the established requirements.

Source : Eco-lighthouse Foundation (2017), www.miljofyrtarn.no/eindex.htm.

Improved environmental management is also in line with the concept of corporate social responsibility (CSR), which is defined by the European Commission as "the responsibility of enterprises for their impacts on society". To fully meet their corporate social responsibility, enterprises should have in place a process to integrate social, environmental, ethical, human rights and consumer concerns into their business operations and core strategy in close collaboration with their stakeholders. CSR guidelines are part of the ISO 26000 standard, which was published in 2010.

SMEs may have lower business incentives to engage in CSR, mainly because there are typically smaller reputational risks for SMEs than for large companies. Still, SMEs have many of the same reasons for engaging in CSR that large companies have. The CSR process for SMEs will depend on the size of the enterprise and the nature of its operations and is likely to be informal.

A brief guidance, based on these best international practices, on adapting EMSs to the needs of SMEs has been elaborated as part of a pilot project in Armenia (Chapter 7).

Sector-specific green certifications

The primary goal of green certification programmes is to increase the market share of their members. In order to make environmental management credentials more relevant to specific economic sectors, business associations in many OECD countries collaborate with environmental authorities to develop green certification brands, many of which target SMEs. The environmental regulator (and, sometimes, local authorities) work jointly with trade bodies to produce ***"green standards" for the sector as well as guidelines on how businesses may "earn" the right to display appropriate signs*** (stickers, posters, etc.) to highlight their environmental practices to their customers. Examples of such programmes can be found in a very wide range of economic sectors, most of which are characterised by direct interface between business and retail customers, allowing SMEs to benefit directly from their improved environmental image.

For example, Ireland's Green Hospitality Programme (under the National Waste Prevention Programme) has been developed to act as an umbrella brand for hospitality-related environmental initiatives, including the Green Hospitality Award, Green Restaurants, and Green Festivals. Formal resource efficiency audits, resource consumption benchmarks, workshops, training and guidance are provided to each participating hotel or restaurant to enable them to develop their own environmental programme and prepare for the different levels of award. Hotels pay for membership, but the fee is partly subsidised by the government. This and other examples of best practices were used to develop a brief guidance on green certification in the hospitality sector in Georgia (Chapter 10).

A similar programme for print shops has been quite popular in France. Created in 1998 by a regional Chamber of Trade and Crafts and since rolled out nationwide, the *Imprim'Vert* label has been awarded to over 1 800 print shops that adhere to a set of good environmental practices such as not using toxic products and secure storage and appropriate disposal of waste. However, environmental compliance is not among the label award criteria.

A "green standard" can also be part of a larger self-regulatory business initiative. One such initiative, the Red Tractor Assurance scheme in England and Wales, is administered by Assured Food Standards – a company owned by the UK farm unions and several agro-industry trade bodies. Originally focused on the food safety issue, Red Tractor Assurance has been extended to cover many environmental aspects of food production (management of pesticides, fertilisers, manure runoff, etc.) across about 80 000 participating farms. Under the "environmental compliance module" for pig and poultry producers, certification bodies collect data on compliance with environmental permits when carrying out audits for the Red Tractor scheme. This helps to decrease the number of Environment Agency visits to farms (to just once every three years) and to cut annual permit charges for farmers.

The green certification scheme should be designed in a way that the business benefits to SMEs outweigh its costs: both the direct costs in terms of fees that must be paid to obtain certification and the indirect costs of staff time to be spent complying with their requirements. It is important to communicate to a broad audience to raise the recognition of the certification, starting at a very early stage of the scheme's development. Trade associations should design marketing and promotional materials which a business could use to display to its customers its "green credentials".

Eco-labels

Whereas green certifications apply to businesses, eco-labels have the same function with respect to products. ***Eco-labelling schemes seek to enable producers to harness consumer demand for environmentally friendly goods*** by displaying a legally protected symbol or logo. If the label has this effect, other producers may respond by improving the environmental performance of their products in order to obtain a label in an attempt to regain the market share. This results in a reduced environmental impact from the products within the product group. The impact of reputational incentives among SMEs is typically lower than among larger enterprises, but they can be effective if they are relevant to local supply chains or customers.

Eco-labelling schemes are generally voluntary: a firm that wishes to have an environmental label awarded to its product may apply to the labelling scheme, and the label will be awarded if the product meets the relevant criteria. ***Eco-label criteria can be based on a single parameter or on studies that analyse the environmental impact of a product or service throughout its life cycle.***

As part of its ISO 14000 series of environmental standards, the International Standards Organisation has drawn up a group of standards specifically governing environmental labelling. The ISO 14020 family covers three types of labelling schemes: Type I is a multi-attribute label developed by a third party; Type II is a single-attribute label developed by the producer; and Type III is an eco-label based on a full life-cycle assessment. Environmental product declarations (EPD) providing quantitative information about a product in a standardised form may also be considered a form of eco-labelling. EPD systems are relatively costly to establish and operate, making SMEs' participation in them unlikely.

Single-attribute labels represent an environmental declaration by an enterprise about a particular environmental characteristic of a product, which in some schemes has to be verified by a third party. Such eco-labels can be related to energy efficiency (for example, the US "Energy Star"), sustainable management of a particular natural resource (e.g. forestry eco-labels), the percentage of recycled material in a product, etc. The simplicity of single-attribute eco-labels makes them particularly attractive to SMEs.

A key feature of lifecycle eco-labels is that an independent third party is involved in assigning the eco-label. Since a product is assessed against a number of approved criteria, the producer is forced to collect and analyse a lot of information that could be used to improve product characteristics through the entire life cycle. The EU Ecolabel, the Scandinavian "Nordic Swan" and the German "Blue Angel" are examples of lifecycle eco-labels.

The effectiveness of eco-labels in motivating enterprises to improve environmental performance depends on criteria defined for a particular product group. ***The environmental criteria need to be updated and made more stringent regularly so that only best products are able to meet them***, thereby ensuring that the eco-label remains a mark of excellence within a product group. Labelling schemes should combat misleading claims by manufacturers about their products.

The proliferation of green labels may create confusion among firms and consumers, particularly since the verification of claims of environmental friendliness is difficult. Sometimes industries create eco-labelling schemes simply to sell themselves to customers, which leads to significant "greenwashing". Therefore, ***the criteria and process for determining whether a product merits an eco-label or green certification should be transparent.*** It is necessary to ensure that labels are not awarded too easily, without rigorous scrutiny of each company's practices.

Eco-labelling schemes are usually run by non-profit organisations (including governments) without commercial interests. To cover their costs, scheme operators commonly an application fee as well as an annual charge, depending on the turnover of the labelled product. The EU Ecolabel scheme, managed by the European Commission since 1992, provides preferential treatment for SMEs, with considerably reduced application and annual fees.

National eco-label schemes may, however, be costly for SMEs to participate in. In Korea, for example, the number of eco-certified products is very large and continues to grow, but the growth of the number of companies producing such products is much slower, which demonstrates the predominant share of larger firms and not of SMEs in the green products market (Figure 4.1). An SME should consider applying for an eco-label if it feels that the expected benefits of doing so (maintaining or increasing its market share) outweigh the costs (those of meeting the eco-label criteria and the scheme charges).

Figure 4.1. **Manufacturing of certified green products in Korea**

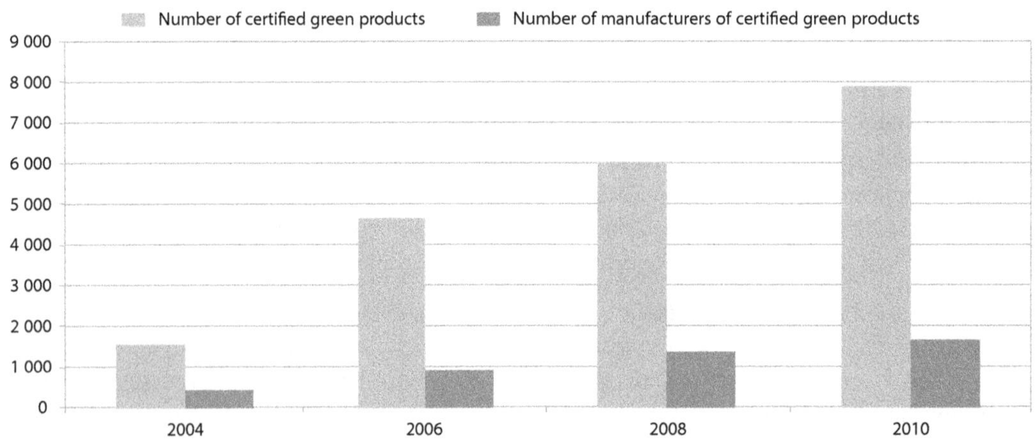

Source: Ministry of Environment of Korea, responses to the OECD questionnaire, February 2012.

Another point that should be stressed is that establishment of national eco-label schemes in small countries often does not pay off because of a limited market and relatively high cost for companies. However, it could be economically and practically feasible to establish a simplified national product certification scheme for particular products widely produced in the country.

Environmental recognition awards

Governments can also use positive public relations incentives to promote environmentally friendly business behaviour. ***Environmental awards help raise environmental awareness through businesses and the community and help companies gain recognition for their good environmental performance.*** For example, the "Vision in Business for the Environment of Scotland" (VIBES) initiative recognises businesses of all sizes and sectors employing environmental best practices in their daily activities. The award programme is supported by the Scottish Environment Protection Agency and run in partnership with other government bodies. It is supported financially through private sponsorship and has in-kind support from a number of business associations. There are several award categories, including Best Environmental Management, Best Environmental Product or Service, Best Co-operation for the Environment, and Best Micro-business Award. A case study is produced for each winning business and published on the VIBES website. The VIBES awards are also used as a mechanism for providing direct advice to applicants via site visits, and further environmental improvements are encouraged via feedback and wide information dissemination.

To be effective, environmental awards need to be widely promoted in business and industry media. However, some SMEs may not have the financial or labour resources to enable them to complete the application process, which may dissuade them from entering environmental awards.

Environmental awards can also recognise the role of different stakeholders in greening small businesses. The US National Steering Committee for the Small Business Ombudsman/Small Business Environmental Assistance Programs has established four Small Business Recognition Awards. Among them, the Trade Association Environmental Leadership Award recognises exemplary performance and leadership by an industry trade organisation in enhancing members' compliance with environmental regulations. There is also an award for a small business environmental assistance programme. The European Enterprise Promotion Awards recognise public bodies and public-private partnerships that support the development of green markets and resource efficiency (EC, 2014b).

Conclusion

Effective communication is a vital component of any greening strategy. To be compliant, SMEs need to know what the regulations are in the first place, and what tools are at their disposal to green their enterprise and be consistent with or exceed their requirements. Both what the message is and what channels are used to communicate needs to be carefully calibrated. The business case for greening SME practices should be emphasised, including the potential commercial benefits (new business opportunities, preferred supplier status, etc.), communication benefits (positive public image, better relationships with customers, investors and regulators), and increased employee motivation and morale. It also needs to be clear who can be contacted for more information – especially important when multiple agencies are involved in different aspects of environmental regulation.

How that information reaches SMEs is as important as what is conveyed. Although internet-based communication is cost-effective, it may not always reach SMEs depending on the sector they are in or the level of technology penetration. Regulatory Watch newsletters can be an effective channel, as can mailings, brochures, and workshops.

The difference between compliance and good practice needs to be clear in the instructions, so that SMEs are aware of both their obligations and the potential to go beyond. Sector-specific communication and training, through public authorities and business associations, is generally much more effective than communication broadly aimed at SMEs as a whole. To be successful, this requires collaboration with industry, gaining credibility and insight into challenges. Non-governmental organisations can also be valuable channels of information and training delivery where appropriate.

Environmental awards, sector specific green certifications and ecolabels all provide ways to recognise and encourage good environmental practices and motivate positive behavior. SMEs benefit as well from potential access to green value chains and broadening market share. Simplified EMS systems also provide a means of recognition and certification, while supporting the SMEs in environmental compliance. To ensure uptake, the cost of certification needs to be less than the potential economic benefits.

Chapter 8 of this Toolkit describes a proposal for the implementation of these instruments in an EaP country-specific context, through an Information Scheme on green practices for SMEs in Moldova. This pilot project was developed at the stakeholders' request. The Scheme involves the Ministries of Economy and Environment, other government agencies, business support organisations and general and sector-specific business associations. It defines the roles and responsibilities of each institutional actor, types of information products to be developed and their general description and target audience, mechanisms of their delivery to the SME community, and procedures for co-ordination between different institutional actors.

Note

1. Businesses acknowledge the value of hearing about enforcement action taken against other businesses in their sector (Defra, 2011a).

References

ACFCI (2010), *Guide PME/PMI Environnement et Énergie*, Édition 2010, Assemblée des Chambres Françaises de Commerce et d'Industrie, Paris.

Calogirou C. et al. (2010), *SMEs and the environment in the European Union*, PLANET S.A. and Danish Technological Institute, Published by European Commission, DG Enterprise and Industry, https://ec.europa.eu/docsroom/documents/13176/attachments/1/translations/en/renditions/pdf.

Defra (2011b), *Micro businesses and environmental regulation*, Final Report prepared by GHK Consulting Ltd. for Defra, Department for Environment, Food and Rural Affairs, http://randd.defra.gov.uk/Document.aspx?Document=Deframicrobusiness_FINALREPORT.pdf.

EC (2014a), *Study on economic and social benefits of environmental protection and resource efficiency related to the European Semester*, Final report for DG Environment, Brussels, https://publications.europa.eu/en/publication-detail/-/publication/ef0c52c7-ed27-4b86-a4c3-e34d1bab4d1c.

EC (2014b), *Green Action Plan for SMEs: Enabling SMEs to turn environmental challenges into business opportunities*, Communication from the Commission to the European Parliament, the Council, the European Economic and Social Committee and the Committee of the Regions, COM(2014)440 Final, Brussels, 2 July 2014, http://ec.europa.eu/growth/smes/business-friendly-environment/green-action-plan/.

EC (2013), *SMEs, Resource Efficiency and Green Markets*, Flash Eurobarometer 381, conducted by TNS Political & Social at the request of Directorate-General Enterprise and Industry, European Commission, Brussels, https://data.europa.eu/euodp/data/dataset/S1086_381.

Eco-lighthouse Foundation (2017), *Eco-lighthouse,* www.eco-lighthouse.org/.

Eftec (2008), *Economic Evaluation of the Benefits of NetRegs to Small and Medium Enterprise Users in the UK: 2008 baseline and future valuation method*, Final Report, Eftec, London, www.netregs.org.uk/media/1104/2009-eftec_netregs_final-report_apr08-2003-format.pdf.

Enterprise Ireland (2015), *Green Offer*, Enterprise Ireland, www.envirocentre.ie.

GreenEcoNet (2015), *GreenEcoNet*, www.greeneconet.eu.

IEEP (2006), *Environmental Compliance Assistance for SMEs: Analysis of Specific Initiatives at National and Local Level and Identification of Best Practices*, Final Report for DG Environment, European Commission, http://ec.europa.eu/environment/archives/sme/pdf/ieep_en.pdf.

NetRegs (2009), *SME-nvironment Survey 2009: UK*, www.netregs.gov.uk (the website discontinued as of October 2011).

OECD (2009), *Ensuring Environmental Compliance: Trends and Good Practices*, Organisation for Economic Co-operation and Development, Paris, www.oecd.org/env/tools-evaluation/ensuringenvironmentalcompliancetrendsandgoodpractices.htm.

SNIFFER (2011), *Description of Regulatory Approaches to Assessing the Effectiveness of Regulatory Activities at Low-risk Sites and Proposed Good Practice Framework*, Final Report, Project ER13, Scotland and Northern Ireland Forum for Environmental Research, Edinburgh, UK, www.fwr.org/environw/er13.htm.

Starkey R., ed. (1998), *Environmental Management Tools for SMEs: A Handbook*, Environmental Issues Series, European Environment Agency, Copenhagen.

Chapter 5

Economic incentives to encourage greening of EaP SMEs

This chapter examines some of the economic tools that governments can use to support the greening of SMEs. This includes tax privileges such as incentives and exemptions. The chapter also examines the role of direct subsidies for consulting services, which can help increase SMEs' awareness and secure their initial engagement in green practices. At the same time, to both ensure the sustainability of practice, as well as the perceived value of the assistance, the chapter also points to the need to gradually shift to a fee-based system for technical assistance. Greening public procurement is also a powerful tool that governments can deploy. The chapter explores how it can impact entire value chains and provide an important lever to support greening. The chapter also notes that while public financial institutions are an important piece of the puzzle, it is also important to enhance the role of private banks and insurance companies in providing incentives for good environmental performance of SMEs, through better loan or insurance policy conditions to businesses with green credentials.

Introduction

Governments have a range of economic tools at their disposal that can be deployed to encourage green practices in SMEs, and support their uptake. These include providing incentives through the tax code to make investing in green technology and more energy efficient equipment financially attractive, creating grants for environmental consulting services and simplified EMS certification, and greening government procurement to encourage supply chain transformation and create a market for green products. This chapter explores those tools and looks at how they have been deployed so far in OECD countries, and what that means for their use in EaP countries.

Tax privileges

Tax privileges are a powerful tool to encourage SMEs to enhance their environmental practices, as well as to support the development of new green enterprises. In many OECD countries, entrepreneurs are allowed to take ***tax exemptions*** and deduct certain categories of environment-related investments from their taxable corporate income. These exemptions are intended to encourage going beyond environmental compliance, and expire after a clearly defined period of time. Often, they are developed in the context of economic policy aimed at promoting innovation, research and development. Similarly, the government may offer ***tax incentives – accelerated depreciation, reduced property or corporate taxes*** – for the purchase of new environmental technologies and other environmental investments. Tax reductions or exemptions can also be differentiated based on the actual environmental impact of the investment.

Box 5.1. **Financial incentives for environmental investments in the Netherlands**

MIA and VAMIL are two separate measures to promote the use of environmental technologies by Dutch companies. Although MIA and VAMIL have been introduced separately in the Netherlands, these measures have many similarities.

VAMIL is a measure enabling a company to freely determine the depreciation period of up to 75% of the cost of the invested environmental technology that is on an official environment ministry listing. Consequently, VAMIL can offer entrepreneurs a financial advantage, as technologies can be depreciated more quickly. Although it is difficult to determine the precise advantage that is gained by using a VAMIL technology – the benefits depend largely on the specific conditions under which the entrepreneurs apply for VAMIL – generally the advantage is estimated between 3 to 8% of the investments made.

MIA enables companies to deduct environmental investments up to 36% of the investment cost. The benefits that can be gained via the MIA scheme depend on the investment and the applied tax scheme (corporate tax or income tax). The percentages of the investment that can be deducted from taxes are explicitly determined and mentioned in the "Environment list". Depending on the investment and applied technology, entrepreneurs can deduct 15, 30 or 40%.

Both schemes are accessible for all business. Yet, 93% of applicants are SMEs, and most of them work in the agricultural sector, as trade associations in this sector are particularly active in encouraging businesses to use this fiscal instrument.

Sources : Lindblom and Delgado (2007), *Promoting Environmental Technologies in SMEs: Barriers and Measures,* http://publications.jrc.ec.europa.eu/repository/bitstream/JRC37214/eur22769en.pdf; ECAP (2011), *Environmental Compliance Assistance Programme for SMEs, Case studies,* http://ec.europa.eu/environment/archives/sme/cases/case_study_en.htm.

For example, the Netherlands has been operating two tax reduction schemes to promote the purchase of new environmental technologies (Box 5.1): the Arbitrary Depreciation of Environmental Investments (VAMIL) allows accelerated depreciation of newly purchased environmental technologies listed by the government, and the Environmental Investment Allowance (MIA) allows a partial write-off of an investment in environmental technology against tax.

The French government uses accelerated depreciation and reduced property and professional taxes to stimulate purchases of renewable energy and energy efficient equipment. The Japanese government provides industry with tax preferences (e.g. reductions in the local corporate tax) for cleaner and climate-friendly technologies (OECD, 2009). However, environmental tax incentive schemes tend to benefit larger companies, which are better informed about the existence of such instruments.

These tax reduction instruments should be complemented by the taxation of negative environmental impacts. Taxes on environmentally harmful products clearly dominate environmentally related taxation in OECD countries (OECD 2014a) and should provide an additional stimulus for SME greening. At the same time, pollution taxes only have an incentive impact if the real pollution is monitored at the source (while under simplified regulation SMEs usually do not have self-monitoring requirements); and the administrative cost of collecting environmental taxes from the multitude of small companies is excessive.

Grants and free consultancy services

Grants may be offered by public agencies for the purchase of environmental technologies (Box 5.2), but more often they ***subsidise a share of consultancy costs for the identification and implementation of resource efficiency and other environmentally oriented measures***. Sometimes the government reimburses SMEs the full cost of an initial environmental audit.

Box 5.2. **Subsidies for environmental technology investments in Belgium**

The Ecology Premium programme in Flanders, Belgium is a subsidy provided to enterprises that invest in environmental technologies. Investments that are considered environmentally friendly are eligible for support as long as they concern purchases from third parties under market conditions.

The size of the subsidy depends on the environmental performance of the technology, measured by an environmental performance factor. This performance factor is a qualitative indication that ranges between 0.6 and 1. The Flemish Department of Economic Support Policy has composed a list of environmental technologies and their performance factors. When a company applies for a subsidy to finance a technology that is not on the list, its potential environmental impact must be assessed.

SMEs can receive a subsidy with a maximum of 35% of the investments made (it can be higher if the company is certified according to ISO 14001 or EMAS) but cannot exceed EUR 3.6 million.

Source : Lindblom and Delgado (2007), *Promoting Environmental Technologies in SMEs: Barriers and Measures*, http://publications.jrc.ec.europa.eu/repository/bitstream/JRC37214/eur22769en.pdf.

For example, Enterprise Ireland, a public industrial development agency, provides grants to SMEs as a percentage (up to 50%) of consultancy costs for the identification and implementation of resource efficiency and other environmentally oriented measures (as long as they go beyond compliance with legal requirements). One enterprise can get up to EUR 200 000 over three years. Grants are associated with compliance audits, which also serve as a compliance assistance tool. France's Environment and Energy Management Agency (ADEME) subsidises up to 50% of the costs of environmental audits, which cover both compliance and resource efficiency. The German public bank *Kreditanstalt für Wiederaufbau* (KfW) has a "Special Fund for Energy Efficiency in SMEs" which covers up to 80% of costs for SMEs to receive professional advice on energy efficiency improvements (Miller, 2011).

In the late 1990s and the early 2000s, many OECD governments provided direct financial support and extensive technical assistance to businesses, especially SMEs, for the establishment and certification of an EMS. For example, the Bavarian Environmental Agreement, launched in 1995 between the *länder* (state) government and industry, allowed SMEs to receive subsidies for an audit by an environmental consultant and the establishment of an EMS (SNIFFER, 2008). Some of these support programmes have now been phased out (e.g. in the Netherlands) as their primary mission to jump-start the market demand for corporate environmental management has been accomplished. Others, like the Green Offer by Enterprise Ireland (Box 4.3), have made the increased competitiveness of national industry an explicit focus of their EMS promotion activities.

Direct subsidies and free technical assistance to SMEs helps to increase their awareness and secure their initial engagement in green practices. However, given the limited availability of public funding for promoting compliance and green business practices, ***a gradual transition toward a fee-based system for technical assistance would improve its long-term sustainability***. This transition would also mean transferring the delivery of technical assistance to trade associations which often charge businesses cost recovery fees for compliance audits, assistance with EMS implementation, training of environmental managers and similar services (see also Section 4.1.4). The dilemma with having small businesses pay for technical assistance is that they may not be able to afford the fees (and often feel that the provision of environmental help and support should be free). At the same time, charging for a fee for services helps alleviate the distrust of free services that businesses have, particularly when they are provided by government agencies.

Role of supply chain management and public procurement

Supply chain pressure offers a valuable means of influencing the environmental behaviour of SMEs. Environmental awareness in global supply chains also affects which suppliers a firm is willing to use, so suppliers receive pressure from buyers to reduce impact. Meeting green quality standards can be challenging for SMEs which face growing pressures to reduce costs, but they also offer SMEs access to environmentally conscious large firms, knowledge flows and global markets.

There are several motivations for large companies to engage in greening the supply chain. Firms with global supply chains and outsourcing strategies are forced to monitor environmental impact to reduce risk: a supplier closed down for poor environmental performance could both disrupt the supply chain and cause serious reputational damage. In addition, better "upstream" environmental performance generates cost savings for larger firms from more efficient production practices.

Increasingly complex supply chains make it difficult to implement and sustain green practices because production is increasingly dispersed across multiple sites and autonomous partnerships. So the whole supply chain needs to engage in green initiatives to gain competitive advantage. ***Supply chain pressure is particularly important and effective in sectors dominated by business-to-business transactions.***

Larger firms often not only require good environmental performance from their suppliers but also work with them to facilitate the improvements. They invest in the environmental capacity of smaller suppliers because without it their own environmental goals cannot be met. The examples include Wal-Mart in the US and Marks & Spencer in the UK. Big Korean companies sign "voluntary green purchasing pacts" with smaller suppliers. Larger companies may also audit their suppliers for resource and energy efficiency, this being primarily a cost-driven measure.

Less formally, sustainable supply chain management may serve to influence suppliers in a more indirect way, if these suppliers improve their production processes in anticipation of gaining new business from a different or broader set of customers demanding sustainable products. Buyers' pressure and support are especially important for small suppliers who lack internal capabilities to proactively define their own greening strategy (OECD, 2012).

The government should encourage larger firms to form partnerships with smaller suppliers and provide public recognition to those who do so. For example, a Business-to-Business Green Mentor Programme was launched in 2003 by the Limerick/Clare/Kerry Regional Waste Management Office in Ireland. It urges larger good practice companies to provide guidance on waste prevention to SMEs. Programme activities include an informational visit by SMEs to a volunteer "mentor" company, with follow-up guidance for individual SMEs on how to identify and implement ways of reducing waste generation or energy or water consumption. In another example, Zero Waste Scotland concludes voluntary agreements with retail companies that then pass on the resource efficiency requirements down the supply chain.

Governments can exert its own supply chain pressure through its procurement policies. Green public procurement (GPP) can play a significant role in creating demand for green products and services and boosting the market where private consumer demand for them is insufficient. By using their purchasing power to choose goods and services with lower environmental impact, public authorities can help to drive down the costs of such purchases and make them more affordable generally. Green public procurement also increases market acceptance of green products (e.g. by demonstrating their commercial feasibility). Countries increasingly recognise that GPP can also be a major driver for innovation, providing industry with incentives for developing green products and services, particularly in sectors where public purchasers represent a large share of the market (e.g. construction, health services and public transport).

GPP makes it a condition of tendering for government contracts that the applicant commit to maintaining specified environmental standards up and down the supply chain. Green procurement may also take the form of exclusion criteria, where only firms certified to a recognised environmental standard are allowed to be considered, or assessment criteria, where a firm's environmental performance is scored on a scale, and the result if part of the procurement decision.

GPP guidelines often require that particular products contain a minimum amount of recycled content or achieve specified levels of energy efficiency. Purchasing guidelines may also favour – through price preferences, explicit set-asides, or other mechanisms – suppliers who comply with environmental requirements, obtain green certification, qualify for environmental labels, or otherwise demonstrate their environmental credentials. GPP most often covers areas such as the purchase of energy-efficient computers and appliances, environmentally-designed buildings, recycled paper, electric cars, and electricity from renewable energy sources. Irish EPA's Green Procurement Guidance for the Public Sector went even further and targeted several additional areas: food and catering services, cleaning products and services, and uniforms and other textiles (EPA, 2014).

OECD governments at the national, regional and local levels increasingly include environmental criteria in their purchasing decisions. The 2002 OECD Council recommendation to improve the environmental performance of public procurement (Box 5.3) reflected their commitment to such practices. The European Commission has proposed that 50% of all public tenders in the member states be "green", i.e. compliant with common core Green Public Procurement criteria.[1] The 2010 OECD Survey on Public Procurement found that 26 out of 34 OECD member countries have introduced practical guides on green public procurement, and 19 countries have developed training materials for public officials on green procurement (OECD, 2014b).

Box 5.3. OECD recommendation on the environmental performance in public procurement

As part of the Recommendation on the Environmental Performance in Public Procurement, OECD countries committed taking steps to:

- provide the appropriate policy framework to incorporate environmental criteria into public procurement of products and services, along with price and performance criteria
- introduce financial, budgeting, and accounting measures to ensure that public procurement policies and practices consider the environmental costs of products and services
- provide information, training and technical assistance to officials involved in the public procurement and use chain, including those who set the performance criteria of products and services, those who are responsible for procurement, and those who use the products and services
- make information and tools that facilitate greener public purchasing available to all levels of government
- disseminate the information needed to facilitate and encourage greener public purchasing decisions, as well as the results and benefits derived from their adoption
- Establish procedures for the identification of products and services which meet the objectives of greener public purchasing policies
- encourage the development of indicators to measure and monitor progress made in greener public purchasing
- assess and evaluate greener public purchasing policies in order to ensure that they are economically efficient and environmentally effective.

Source : OECD (2002), *Council Recommendation on Improving the Environmental Performance of Public Procurement*, https://legalinstruments.oecd.org/Instruments/ShowInstrumentView.aspx?InstrumentID=46&Lang=en&Book=False.

For example, the Scottish Government's "Public Procurement and Sustainable Development: Guidelines for Public Purchasers"[2] states that "those who fail to comply with environmental legislation may be excluded from selling to the Scottish Government" and that "development of environmentally preferable goods and services and use of recycled/renewable materials is likely to offer a competitive advantage". The Scottish Government also seeks evidence that suppliers have in place appropriate environmental management policies and systems. In addition, suppliers are encouraged to take advantage of eco-labelling schemes to be able to provide evidence of their good environmental practices. UK Defra has gone even further, encouraging suppliers to provide product-level lifecycle greenhouse gas data using emission factors from relevant inventory databases.

The US Federal Government requires that 95% of all government contracts meet sustainability requirements. Its ambition is that environmental considerations become part of normal procurement practice along with such traditional factors as product safety, price, performance and availability (OECD, 2013).

Procurement policies co-ordinated across all levels of government may directly affect, on average, up to 20% of purchases in a targeted market (OECD, 2003). As shown in Figure 5.1, public purchasing of environmentally-friendly goods and services in Korea helped jump-start the private sector market for them, whose growth rate has quickly outstripped the expansion of green public procurement.

Figure 5.1. **Size of the green product market and public procurement in Korea**

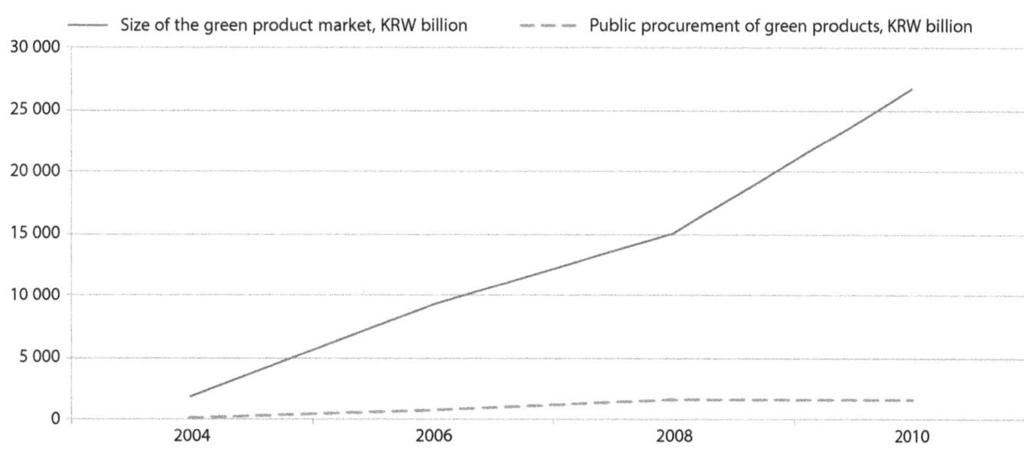

Note: EUR 1 equalled approximately KRW 1 480 in February 2012.

Source: Ministry of Environment of Korea, responses to the OECD questionnaire, February 2012.

Although the vast majority of public sector contracts go to large firms, public procurement is a big issue for SMEs because for many of them public contracts represent a significant share of business. Several OECD countries (e.g. Australia, France, Korea and the US) give preference to SMEs in public procurement (OECD, 2011). Still, only one out of ten EU SMEs bid for public procurement contracts that include environmental requirements versus 16% of large companies (EC, 2012). In a recent Eurobarometer SME survey, just 12% of SMEs in the EU report to have bid for a public procurement tender that included environmental requirements. More than half of SMEs have never been confronted with such a tender (EC, 2013).

To reach SMEs, governments should communicate their green purchasing policy to a wide range of stakeholders, including present and future suppliers, service providers or contractors, so that they can take account of the new requirements. They should also educate procurement officials on how to implement these policies. The target group for educational activities can be contracting authorities of central administration bodies and their subordinated organisations, at the level of regional governments and local authorities. These activities should include dissemination of technical information on GPP and related issues, such as eco-labelling, environmental management systems and energy labelling.

Conclusion

The government has a range of tools at its disposal to create economic incentives for SMEs to go beyond the minimum environmental compliance requirements. At their base, they all come down to the same thing: ensuring that it makes economic sense for SMEs to undertake changes to improve their environmental performance. Tax exemptions and incentives lessen the short-term costs of investing in greener practices. Grants and subsidisation of consultancy costs helps SMEs identify and implement more resource efficient and environmentally practices. Putting green requirements into government procurement helps create market incentives for greener practices, both for SMEs who are directly participating in government procurement, and those who are participating in the supply chain of larger companies. This supply chain pressure is particularly important in industries that are business-to-business, rather than customer facing.

Notes

1. www.ec.europa.eu/environment/gpp/gpp_criteria_en.htm.
2. www.gov.scot/Publications/2009/10/sspap.

References

EC (2013), *SMEs, Resource Efficiency and Green Markets*, Flash Eurobarometer 381, conducted by TNS Political & Social at the request of Directorate-General Enterprise and Industry, European Commission, Brussels, https://data.europa.eu/euodp/data/dataset/S1086_381.

EC (2012), *SMEs, Resource Efficiency and Green Markets*, Flash Eurobarometer 342, conducted by TNS Political & Social at the request of Directorate-General Enterprise and Industry, European Commission, Brussels, ec.europa.eu/commfrontoffice/publicopinion/flash/fl_342_en.pdf.

EC (2004a), *Buying Green!* A handbook on environmental public procurement, European Commission, http://ec.europa.eu/environment/gpp/pdf/Buying-Green-Handbook-3rd-Edition.pdf.

ECAP (2011), *Environmental Compliance Assistance Programme for SMEs, Case studies*, http://ec.europa.eu/environment/archives/sme/cases/case_study_en.htm, accessed 12 August 2011.

EPA (2014), *Green Procurement Guide for the Public Sector*, Environmental Protection Agency, Ireland, www.epa.ie/pubs/advice/green%20business/GreenPublicProcurementfinalwebv2.pdf.

Lindblom, J. and L. Delgado, eds. (2007), *Promoting Environmental Technologies in SMEs: Barriers and Measures*, Institute for Prospective Technological Studies, DG Joint Research Centre, European Commission, Seville, Spain, http://publications.jrc.ec.europa.eu/repository/bitstream/JRC37214/eur22769en.pdf.

Miller, K. et al. (2011), *First Assessment of the Environmental Assistance Programme for SMEs (ECAP)*, Final report, prepared by AEA Technology Plc. for the European Commission, DG Environmental and Climate Action, London, http://ec.europa.eu/environment/archives/sme/pdf/First%20assessemnt%20of%20the%20ECAP%20for%20SMEs.pdf.

OECD (2014a), *Creating Market Incentives for Greener Products: Policy Manual for Eastern Partnership Countries,* Organisation for Economic Co-operation and Development, Paris, www.oecd.org/environment/outreach/economic-instruments.htm.

OECD (2014b), *Going Green: Best Practices for Green Procurement*, Public Governance Committee, GOV/PGC/ETH(2014)1/REV1, August 2014, Organisation for Economic Co-operation and Development, Paris, www2.oecd.org/oecdinfo/info.aspx?app=OLIScoteEN&Ref=GOV/PGC/ETH(2014)1/REV1.

OECD (2013), *Mapping out good practices for promoting green public procurement*, Public Governance Committee, GOV/PGC/ETH(2013)3, January 2013, Organisation for Economic Co-operation and Development, Paris, www2.oecd.org/oecdinfo/info.aspx?app=OLIScoteEN&Ref=GOV/PGC/ETH(2013)3.

OECD (2012), *Green Entrepreneurship, Eco-innovation and SMEs*, Working Party on SMEs and Entrepreneurship, CFE/SME(2011)9/REV1, April 2012, Organisation for Economic Co-operation and Development, Paris, www.oecd.org/officialdocuments/publicdisplaydocumentpdf/?cote=CFE/SME(2011)9/FINAL&docLanguage=En.

OECD (2011), *Government at a Glance*, Organisation for Economic Co-operation and Development, Paris, www.oecd.org/gov/governmentataglance2011.htm.

OECD (2009), *Ensuring Environmental Compliance: Trends and Good Practices*, Organisation for Economic Co-operation and Development, Paris, www.oecd.org/env/tools-evaluation/ensuringenvironmentalcompliancetrendsandgoodpractices.htm.

OECD (2003), *The Environmental Performance of Public Procurement: Issues of Policy Coherence*, Organisation for Economic Co-operation and Development, Paris, www.oecd-ilibrary.org/environment/the-environmental-performance-of-public-procurement_9789264101562-en.

OECD (2002), *Council Recommendation on Improving the Environmental Performance of Public Procurement*, C(2002)3, Organisation for Economic Co-operation and Development, Paris, https://legalinstruments.oecd.org/Instruments/ShowInstrumentView.aspx?InstrumentID=46&Lang=en&Book=False.

SNIFFER (2008), *Better Regulation – Rethinking the Approach for SMEs*, Final Report, Project UKCC19, Scotland and Northern Ireland Forum for Environmental Research, Edinburgh, UK, www.fwr.org/waterq/ukcc19.htm.

Chapter 6

Institutional aspects of greening SMEs in EaP countries

This chapter looks at the institutional structures that EaP countries need to establish in order to support the greening of SMEs. It begins with a discussion of the need to build the capacity of government actors, especially local and regional government administrations, to help signpost SMEs to where they can get appropriate resources and information (if it is not available at the local level). The role of national environmental authorities in overall co-ordination of efforts to promote green activity of SMEs is also noted. The chapter then discusses the vital place of trade associations and other industry groups in supporting greening efforts, as they are most likely to have effective communication channels with both their members and government authorities. Finally, the chapter addresses the potential role of financial advisors such as accountants, banks and insurance companies. SMEs are regularly in contact with them, and they are a trusted source of information; they could potentially increase awareness of changes to environmental requirements as well as sources for further information.

Introduction

The best planned environmental regulatory regimes, support programmes, and green economic incentives will not be effective if they are not supported by a strong institutional foundation. This means a clear delineation of who is responsible for supporting greening SMEs, and central anchors that can pull together other information sources and help SMEs navigate through it. It also implies having strong links with industry and non-governmental organisations, which are often vital in supporting greening initiatives. This chapter will explore how OECD countries have been approaching these issues, and how EaP countries can strengthen institutional support for greening SMEs.

Building capacity of government actors in environmental outreach to SMEs

Small businesses get environmental advice and guidance from a multitude of sources, including regulatory agencies, local authorities, special business support organisations, trade or professional associations, consultants, banks and accountants, other business owners and even personal networks (which is especially true for micro-businesses).

A survey of Scottish businesses (NetRegs, 2009) found that almost 70% of businesses managers contact their local government to discuss environmental issues, while less than 30% turn to the national environmental authority. Less than 15% of businesses tend to turn to consultants, trade bodies, business support organisations or a compliance assistance website. These results are similar to those obtained by another UK research (SNIFFER, 2008), which concluded that SMEs looking for information on environmental issues would most likely contact the local authority in the first instance, followed by trade associations, the internet, and professional advisors.

Environmental authorities have regulatory competency over only part of the SME community, and they are not the primary interlocutors of small businesses. However, in OECD countries they often ***co-ordinate efforts of other public and private actors to promote green behaviour of SMEs*** because this role is complementary to their main regulatory function (Box 6.1). To be effective in this co-ordinating role, the environmental authority should:

- build better understanding among its own staff of the diversity, needs and most effective ways to work with SMEs;
- conduct staff training programmes on promoting compliance and resource efficiency;
- better integrate advice into its core compliance monitoring and enforcement activities;
- establish partnerships with other government agencies, local governments, publicly funded business support organisations and business associations to increase its credibility with SMEs and reduce their mistrust;
- explore ways to co-ordinate and leverage resources of other government agencies for developing and implementing innovative approaches to assist the SME community
- enhance interaction with business associations to develop plain language guidance documents and factsheets on environmental compliance and green practices and create opportunities for small businesses to comment on proposed regulations.

While many environmental authorities in OECD countries see developing the ability of their staff to understand the nature and needs of the SMEs that they regulate as a priority area in improving SME compliance, others, especially in EaP countries, have reservations about their role in assisting the regulated community. This is why in the EaP region this role is increasingly being assumed by ministries of economy and the business support organisations created under their auspices.

It is very important that one governmental authority take the lead in establishing a network of actors engaged in helping SMEs improve their environmental performance. Once such a network has been created, its member institutions should perform the crucial "signposting" function of providing businesses with references to direct operators of multiple governmental and non-governmental programmes promoting different aspects of green business. One example of such effort is the "Green Who?" guide for businesses on green supports on offer that has been developed by the Irish EPA. Environmental inspectors should have checklists and reminders to refer operators to appropriate assistance providers as part of their compliance monitoring routine.

In countries where local governments play an important role in regulating small businesses, ***the national government should work with local authorities so that they in turn engage the SME community***. Local authorities in small neighbouring communities may benefit from pooling resources for compliance promotion activities. This could be one of the functions of inter-municipal environmental agencies (also known as joint environmental services) – a model increasingly used in several European countries (e.g. in the Netherlands, Sweden and the UK) for local environmental inspection and enforcement programmes. Ireland represents an example of horizontal collaboration between local authorities in providing compliance assistance: each local authority has an environmental awareness officer who participates in a national network.

Box 6.1. **Institutional network for SME environmental compliance assistance in the United States**

The US Environmental Protection Agency (EPA) has over the years established an extensive network of thousands of public and private compliance assistance providers in different states and industrial sectors. The EPA Office of Compliance has provided technical and financial support to compliance assistance providers which include federal and state regulators, trade associations, as well as universities, non-profit organisations and consulting firms.

In an effort to help encourage better communication around the country between the EPA and state technical assistance programmes, a National Steering Committee (for the state Small Business Ombudsman and Small Business Environmental Assistance Programs) and a National Compliance Advisory Panel (for the state compliance advisory panels, or CAPs) have been formed. Through these co-ordinated efforts, state programmes are able to tackle issues relevant to their purpose and share information to help avoid duplication of effort.

States commonly receive federal grants for compliance promotion activities but use them in accordance with their own priorities. Each state CAP reviews and renders advisory opinions on its state's assistance programme, ensures that information affecting small businesses is written in a clear and understandable style, and serves as an information bridge between small businesses and the state's environmental regulator. Some states (such as California, New Jersey and Pennsylvania) have a separate, high-level compliance assistance office.

Source : OECD (2009), *Ensuring Environmental Compliance: Trends and Good Practices*, www.oecd.org/env/tools-evaluation/ensuringenvironmentalcompliancetrendsandgoodpractices.htm.

Involvement of trade associations and other business groups

Business and trade associations tend to have well-established communication channels with their members and with governments, and an understanding the regulatory challenges faced by their members and the approaches that work best for them. Most OECD country governments work with business and trade associations to explain new environmental regulations to their members, as well as to provide regulators with practical support in designing regulatory approaches to address sector-specific needs. However, only in a few countries do they use trade associations to stimulate directly the adoption of green practices.

At the same time, evidence suggests the potential value of increased engagement of business and trade associations in promoting green behaviour of small businesses. In a recent survey of European SMEs (EC, 2013), businesses indicated that external support for green practices was much more likely to come from the private rather than the public sector (75% vs. 35%). Advice and other non-financial assistance from private companies (43%) and business associations (36%) were quoted as the most common forms of external support.

Working in partnership with business groups can be particularly useful as SMEs can be apprehensive about outreach activities from regulatory agencies. ***Business and trade associations have a role to play in "signposting" different web-based information and guidance sources*** and communicating their usefulness for small businesses given SMEs' reluctance to proactively seek such information on the internet. Feedback from businesses groups is extremely useful in developing and improving compliance assistance programmes.

Business associations can help small businesses to improve profitability through environmental management, e.g. by ***developing marketing and promotional materials*** which a business could use to display to its customers its "green credentials" and practices. For example, the Bright Green Business Network – a Scotland-wide organisation with fee-based membership – helps its members (mostly SMEs) to find green suppliers, to develop growth opportunities on the basis of good environmental performance.

Business organisations can also have a role in providing ***sector-specific technical assistance to companies introducing green practices*** (through information dissemination, training and referral to sources of expertise). This role in France is played by 21 Technical Industrial Centres (www.reseau-cti.com) covering 32 industry sectors (primarily dominated by SMEs), working with support from different trade associations and funded through fees paid by businesses. However, they face strong competition from private service providers. When a private sector market for environmental assistance services becomes strong enough, it makes sense for such business organisations to phase out direct assistance and keep signposting as the only promotion function.

At the same time, there are certain constraints in engaging business associations in promoting green practices among SMEs. Many membership associations are focused more on defending their members' interests in the design of regulatory requirements and much less on providing them with environmental information and guidance. ***Given the institutional weakness of business associations in EaP countries, they should be a primary target for building capacity in promoting green practices.***

Furthermore, the extensive use of trade associations may be unfeasible if the majority of small businesses do not belong to any such association, which is the case in EaP countries. The initial step would then be to ***explain to SMEs, through a public relations campaign, the benefits of trade associations to their members*** (Box 6.2). In the meantime, the government should rely primarily on state-funded business support organisations, work with trade associations with an already established SME audience, and try to engage other sector groups in more active environmental outreach.

Box 6.2. **Potential benefits of trade associations to SMEs**

There are many potential benefits for businesses to join trade associations, especially for SMEs. Of course, not all trade associations are created equal, and they may themselves require support to develop their capacities. Depending on the level of development, associations can provide:

- free advice on many technical, legal and commercial nature issues, reports on market conditions and trends in the sector, and reduced-rate consultancy services, among other services
- a stronger voice for the sector than individual businesses. As the membership base grows, so does the trade association's authority
- peer networking opportunities for members at conferences, exhibitions and other events while they are learning about issues which may affect their business
- updates regarding changes in industry technical standards, policy and news which are disseminated to members and provide an early warning system with advice on how to deal with the issues which may be encountered as a result
- enhancement of a company's reputation. For many industries, membership of the industry association is seen as a badge of quality, particularly for those industries which are heavily regulated.

Source : Trade Association Forum (2015), www.taforum.org.

Companies willing to improve their environmental performance may also want to create "eco-industrial networks" – partnerships outside the framework of trade associations. An eco-industrial network is more than an informal association of companies: it is intended to be a lasting arrangement in which participating businesses share environmental and cost-effectiveness information. Eco-industrial networks vary greatly in scale and purpose: some may simply share information on new technologies, legislation or training opportunities; others may create functional links among participating companies (e.g. waste management facilities). Such networks are often managed by steering committees which include representatives of national and local government authorities.

Ireland's "Saving Money through Industry Links and Exchanges" (SMILE) Resource Exchange (www.smileexchange.ie) is one such network. It a free service for businesses that encourages the sharing and exchange of resources in order to reduce costs and help the environment. Based on the concept "one's waste could be another's resource", businesses have opportunities to identify potential partnerships through networking exchange events and an online exchange facility. This service is funded by the Irish EPA, Cork County and City Councils, as well as county and city enterprise boards. Eco-industrial networks are also quite popular in Canada, Germany and a few other OECD countries (O'Regan and Moles, 2009). In addition, environmental trade fairs and exhibitions are important venues for networking between small businesses.

A network can also bring together publicly and privately funded business support organisations. The Enterprise Europe Network (EEN) funded by the European Commission brings together close to 600 member organisations, including chambers of commerce and industry, technology centres, universities and development agencies. Focusing on eight industry sectors, it promotes partnerships between public and private organisations as well as SME associations in order to raise SMEs' awareness of their environmental impact, existing and new environmental legislation, and the benefits of environmental management systems (Miller, 2011).

Enhancing the role of banks, accounting and insurance companies

Most SMEs have frequent interaction with accountants, banks and insurance companies and rely on them as credible sources of information. These communication channels provide opportunities for using respective institutions both to disseminate information and to exert pressure on SMEs to pursue environmental improvements to achieve greater business success.

Several studies conducted in the UK have shown that the "most trusted adviser" for SMEs is their accountant (Spence et al., 2012). Accountants routinely give advice to their SME clients on a wide range of topics, including taxation and financial management, but also organisational issues, marketing and strategic planning. There is potential for further widening advice provision to include green practices. To build on this potential, ***the government should work with professional bodies such as accounting associations*** to provide their members with:

- awareness of potential information sources on green practices (including relevant regulatory requirements)
- education to understand specific environmental issues for business, such as the benefits of resource efficiency
- knowledge of the SME aspects of environmental management systems and industry-specific voluntary environmental standards
- training in specific environmental accounting techniques (e.g. environmental auditing skills).

Banks and insurance companies also play an increasingly important role in greening business behaviour. At the international level, the United Nations Environment Programme has published high-profile policy documents to promote sustainability in the banking and insurance sectors (UNEP, 2011, 2012). On the ground, the growing number of large financing institutions follow the Equator Principles for assessing environmental and social risks of project finance transactions (Box 6.3). Banks increasingly require an environmental checklist for loan approval, while insurers demand a statement of environmental risk identification and control.

Governments should actively encourage banks and insurers to offer better loan or insurance policy conditions to businesses with green credentials. Many insurance companies have recognised their own benefits in having client firms that proactively manage their environmental performance, as this leads to reduced levels of risk of insurance claims based on environmental damage. For example, the Irish EPA has started discussions with the Irish Insurance Federation to try to make sure that insurance companies introduce environmental requirements for their clients. Similarly, insurance companies in Korea are considering the differentiation of insurance premiums depending on the level of environmental risk.

Box 6.3. The Equator Principles

The Equator Principles (EPs) are a credit risk management framework for determining, assessing and managing environmental and social risk in project financing. The first three Principles lay down the fundamentals of environmental and social assessment:

Principle 1: Review and Categorisation. When a project is proposed for financing, the financing institution (FI) will, as part of its internal environmental and social review and due diligence, categorise it based on the magnitude of its potential environmental and social risks and impacts.

Principle 2: Environmental and Social Assessment. For all projects with a potential adverse environmental and social impact, the FI will require the client to conduct an assessment of environmental and social risks. The assessment documentation should propose measures to minimise, mitigate, and offset adverse impacts in a manner relevant and appropriate to the nature and scale of the proposed project.

Principle 3: Applicable Environmental and Social Standards. The assessment process should address compliance with relevant host country laws, regulations and permits that pertain to environmental and social issues.

The EPs are adopted voluntarily by FIs and are intended to serve as a common baseline and framework for the implementation by their own internal, social and environmental policies, procedures and standards related to their project financing activities.

Source : Equator Principles (2015), www.equator-principles.com.

Conclusion

It is important that a national government body such as the environment ministry or the ministry of economy take the lead in establishing a network of actors engaged in helping SMEs improve their environmental performance. Once such a network has been created, its member institutions should perform the crucial "signposting" function of providing businesses with references to direct operators of multiple governmental and non-governmental programmes promoting different aspects of green business. Working in partnership with business groups can be particularly useful in developing and improving compliance assistance programmes. Business associations can also help small businesses to improve profitability through better environmental management. Other more general business service providers, such as insurance agents, accountants, and banks, can also act as important conduits for information. They are in regular contact with SMEs.

Overall, the through line in this chapter is the multifaceted nature of institutional support for greening SMEs, and the need to ensure co-ordination and communication among disparate actors. Government support is important, but responsibility for different aspects of environmental regulation sometimes dispersed over different agencies, a national body needs to act to co-ordinate. At the same time, with SMEs often seeking out information from local government, capacity at the local level needs to exist to at the very minimum direct SMEs to where useful resources and information can be found. Finally, as noted above, business associations and private service providers also need to be involved as vital conduits for information.

References

EC (2013), *SMEs, Resource Efficiency and Green Markets*, Flash Eurobarometer 381, conducted by TNS Political & Social at the request of Directorate-General Enterprise and Industry, European Commission, Brussels, https://data.europa.eu/euodp/data/dataset/S1086_381.

Miller, K. et al. (2011), *First Assessment of the Environmental Assistance Programme for SMEs (ECAP)*, Final report, prepared by AEA Technology Plc. for the European Commission, DG Environmental and Climate Action, London, http://ec.europa.eu/environment/archives/sme/pdf/First%20assessemnt%20of%20the%20ECAP%20for%20SMEs.pdf.

NetRegs (2009), *SME-nvironment Survey 2009: UK*, www.netregs.gov.uk (the website discontinued as of October 2011).

OECD (2009), *Ensuring Environmental Compliance: Trends and Good Practices*, Organisation for Economic Co-operation and Development, Paris, www.oecd.org/env/tools-evaluation/ensuringenvironmentalcompliancetrendsandgoodpractices.htm.

O'Regan, B. and R. Moles (2009), *Establishing an Eco-Industrial Network for Small and Medium-Sized Enterprises in the Mid-West Region*, STRIVE Report 2004-SD-MS-19, prepared for the Environmental Protection Agency by Centre for Environmental Research, University of Limerick, Ireland, http://erc.epa.ie/safer/iso19115/displayISO19115.jsp?isoID=104.

SNIFFER (2008), *Better Regulation – Rethinking the Approach for SMEs*, Final Report, Project UKCC19, Scotland and Northern Ireland Forum for Environmental Research, Edinburgh, UK, www.fwr.org/waterq/ukcc19.htm.

Spence, L. et al. (2012), *Environmental aspects of sustainability: SMEs and the role of the accountant*, Research report 128, Association of Chartered Certified Accountants, London, https://research-repository.st-andrews.ac.uk/handle/10023/3776.

UNEP (2012), Principles for Sustainable Insurance, UNEP Finance Initiative, United Nations Environment Programme, Geneva, Switzerland, www.unepfi.org/psi/wp-content/uploads/2012/06/PSI-document1.pdf.

UNEP (2011), UNEP FI Guide to Banking & Sustainability, UNEP Finance Initiative, United Nations Environment Programme, Geneva, Switzerland, www.unepfi.org/fileadmin/documents/guide_banking_statements.pdf.

Chapter 7

Financing for greening SMEs

This chapter examines different strategies to support enhancing the availability finance for greening SMEs in EaP countries. It highlights the importance of access to finance as an enabler for SMEs to take advantage of opportunities to improve their environmental performance. Finance is also important for start-ups that are developing or introducing new green technology. The current situation of green finance in EaP countries is explored, as is the role of public financial institutions' diversity. Green asset-based finance, soft loans, green microfinance, and green bonds are also briefly addressed.

Introduction

In most countries, small and medium sized enterprises (SMEs) face greater challenges to access finance than larger enterprises. SMEs may find interest rates and collateral requirements of bank loans prohibitive, and may not be familiar with other sources of finance that are available. The size and sophistication of both the SMEs and the finance sector can also make the struggle more difficult, as lenders may not have the capacity to address the challenges that SMEs face as opposed to larger enterprises, and may be less interested in lending to smaller enterprises.

The situation is further compounded for green SMEs and SMEs looking to invest in greener practices. Better access to finance can greatly facilitate SMEs' green initiatives, and, for green start-ups, support the development and expansion of their enterprise. However, it can be challenging to make the case to banks, which remain the main source of SME finance beyond internal funds. SMEs may struggle with having the best information to present to lending parties, both in terms of the initial case for the green investment as well as for ongoing reporting. They may find short-term tenors challenging when contrasted against the longer payback periods of some green investments. Institutions are often unfamiliar with valuing the economic benefits of green initiatives, and may be reluctant to provide loans.

However, there are tools and approaches which can support access to green finance for SMEs, approaches that have been successful in the context of SMEs and sustainable finance more broadly. In the aftermath of COP21 and other international discussions on climate change and green growth, there is a global consensus on the need to make finance available for green infrastructure and industry. Increasingly, international financial institutions (IFIs) have dedicated funds specifically for SMEs. It is not simply a question of money being available – SMEs need to have the tools to access affordable (long-term, low-cost) finance, and risk needs to be addressed appropriately. Risk mitigation instruments are an important part of the puzzle as capital remains too expensive for many SMEs. This chapter will examine the challenges facing SMEs seeking green finance, and consider some examples of what has worked in countries both within and without the Eastern Partnership (EaP) region.

Green finance for SMEs in EaP countries

Most commonly, private financing plays a large role in supporting resource efficiency and in the production of green goods and services in EaP countries, compared to public grants and loan guarantees. For SMEs both in OECD countries and the EaP region, internal SME funds remain the most common source of finance for greening initiatives. Beyond that, bank finance is the primary source of external funds for SMEs. which comes mostly in the form of finance by International Finance Institutions (IFIs) that extend green credit lines through local financial institutions (Box 7.1). Almost all IFIs active in EaP countries have opened such credit lines. These include the European Bank for Reconstruction and Development (EBRD), the International Finance Corporation (IFC), the European Investment Bank (EIB), the Asian Development Bank (ADB), the German public bank *Kreditanstalt für Wiederaufbau* (*KfW*), and the Development Bank of Austria (Box 7.1).

A number of IFIs, such as EIB and ADB, provide funding for relevant environmental activities through credit lines primarily dedicated to SMEs. In addition, there are a number of multilateral and bilateral facilities that have also extended environmental credit lines to local financial institutions in the region that target SMEs, such as the Green for Growth Fund and the Global Climate Partnership Fund (OECD 2016a, 2016b).

Box 7.1. **Examples of financing sources for energy efficiency and renewable energy in Armenia**

- Inecobank and Araratbank are providing "green loans" for energy saving projects, including energy-efficient lighting, heat insulation, installation of thermal solar systems, etc. These loans are provided with the support of the Green for Growth Fund for Southeast Europe.
- Ameriabank (since 2012) and Anelik bank (since 2010) are providing "renewable energy loans" under the Armenian Sustainable Energy Financing Facility initiated by the EBRD, aiming to support financing of energy efficiency and renewable energy projects of private business in Armenia.
- IFC provided USD 15 million financing to HSBC Bank Armenia to help the bank support sustainable energy projects and provide loans to SMEs interested in investing in energy efficient technologies and promoting the efficient use of resources.

Source : OECD (2015a), *Promoting better environmental performance of small and medium-sized enterprises in Armenia*, www.oecd.org/environment/outreach/SME-greening-country-pilot-report-Armenia-en.pdf.

Recently, domestic finance institutions have begun to play a growing role. For example in 2013, Moldova's ProCredit Bank launched an EcoLoan programme for business clients, becoming one of the country's first banks to provide "green" loans to small and micro-enterprises for investments in energy efficiency (with required energy savings of at least 20%), renewable energy, and other green practices (organic agriculture, water and soil protection, etc.). ProCredit Bank Georgia operates a similar programme and is itself ISO 14001:2015 certified (OECD 2017-forthcoming).A few banks have established environmental management units, and two banks in Georgia, JSC Bank of Georgia and JSC TBC Bank, have formally adopted environmental and social policies and respective procedures. In some countries, green financing is supported by public interventions, such as the example in the Lviv region of Ukraine where the regional government subsidises interest rates of commercial loans for energy efficiency projects in partnership with five private banks.

Building the capacity of SMEs and lenders

Ensuring that SMEs have access to green finance requires not just ensuring that funds are available, but also building the capacity of different parties when it comes to sustainable investment. As green finance for SMEs is an emerging area of finance, there is often a gap in expertise on both sides of the table. Providing SMEs' with capacity training to make a business case for investments that make their operations more resource efficient or environmentally friendly is important. Equally, financial institutions need to be supported so that they are better equipped to assess the risk and rewards of green investments, and thus put realistic judgements of interest rates. The funds deployed by IFIs through local intermediaries, such as those mentioned in Box 7.1, often include technical capacity as part of the loan programme. For example, since 2006, EBRD's project "Identification and promotion of energy efficiency investments" has combined the provision of credit lines through financial institutions in Moldova and Ukraine with legal, technical, financial and environmental technical assistance to potential beneficiaries (EU 2017). Governments can further enhance this by working through other channels such as local business associations and municipal governments to reach SMEs and ensure that they are informed about the availability of finance options and have the technical knowhow to make the case for initiatives.

The role of public financial institutions

Public financial institutions, local and international, may offer reduced interest loans for environmental investments by SMEs. Such loans are usually conditional on the planned measures going beyond regulatory requirements and the use of best available techniques and/or best environmental management practices, and applications need to be certified by the competent environmental authority (Box 7.2). There are programmes that allow loans to be converted into grants (i.e. do not have to be paid back) upon demonstration of expected environmental performance.

Box 7.2. Low-interest loans for green investments: Examples from selected countries

France: OSEO public investment bank offers loans at favourable rates and without collateral from EUR 50 000 to EUR 3 million for up to seven years for SMEs who adopt environmentally friendly technologies (with the share of capital costs exceeding 60%) or develop new ones.

UK: The Energy Saving Trust (a UK-wide non-profit organisation) provides zero-interest small business loans of up to GBP 100 000 to help businesses install renewable energy technologies or measures that reduce energy consumption.

USA: In the US state of Virginia, a co-operative agreement between the Department of Environmental Quality and the Department of Business Assistance has allowed the state's small businesses, since the year 2000, to obtain loans of up to USD 50 000 to finance the purchase of equipment to implement voluntary pollution prevention measures or to introduce agricultural best management practices. These loans have an interest rate of 3% with favourable repayment terms based on the borrower's ability to repay and the useful life of the equipment being purchased.

Sources : Energy Saving Trust (2014), www.energysavingtrust.org.uk; ECOS (2012), *2012 State Innovations,* https://www.ecos.org/documents/2012-state-innovations/.

There are not very many domestic public finance institutions in EaP countries that can provide targeted soft loans for environmental investments by SMEs, although Ukraine and Belarus do provide some funds. It would be useful to consider stablishing public green finance institutions (banks or funds), or strengthening functions of existing state institutions, so that they can support specifically green projects at SMEs.

Currently, credit lines extended by IFIs and disbursed through local commercial banks are the main source of long-term financing for environmental investments in the region. Such credit lines facilitate access to longer-term finance and make it more feasible to borrow. This does not mean the funds are necessarily cheaper than ordinary loans (i.e. the interest rates are not subsidised), but the end user and the local bank can often benefit from grant-funded consultancy services and training to develop feasible projects. This helps to reduce the risk to the local banks, making them more willing to lend, and also improves the overall effectiveness of the investment.

Important factors of successful implementation of a soft loan programme for environmental investments include:

- ***early definition of the environmental goals*** to be achieved by each project
- ***inclusion of environmental requirements in the loan agreement*** with a clear definition of environmental measures to be taken and adequate monitoring processes
- ***close monitoring and evaluation by the lending institution*** of the use of funds and of progress in achieving its environmental goals.

The role of co-operative banks

Credit unions, co-operatives and other depositor owned banks are more likely to offer the long-term loans that are most valuable to SMEs, and potentially lower collateral requirements. They also have different strengths in terms of supporting access to finance for green SMEs. Credit unions and other depositor owned banks are more likely to take the time to work with SMEs and be familiar with SMEs in their community, helping to minimise information asymmetries. This is also facilitated by local branch offices, with people from the community at hand (UNEP 2017). This suggests that governments in EaP countries as well as IFIs operating in EaP countries may be able to take advantage these institutions as complements to commercial banks, by offering more flexible financial solutions and using their extensive local networks.

Box 7.3. Measures to support the aggregation of green bonds

Warehousing: This refers to using a single entity – a "financial warehouse" – to aggregate and package loans together so that they can be issues as bonds to investors. IFIs can establish these warehouses in-country.

Standardised contracts: As SMEs often do not have individual credit ratings, simply aggregating loans into green bonds leaves a lot of uncertainty for investors. By setting requirements for standardised loan contracts, governments can ensure that bond issuers are able to supply accurate risk information to investors.

Green covered bonds: Governments can also specify that collateral for covered bonds needs to be provided through green assets. This helps encourage SMEs to invest in green assets, as they can then act as loan collateral to pay for the asset investment.

In Mexico, the IADB has set-up a financial warehouse focusing on funding new investments in energy efficiency. The warehouse, which operates as a Special Purpose Vehicle (SPV), makes a senior credit line of up to USD50 million available to three Energy Service Companies (ESCOS) in order to finance energy efficiency investments among SMEs. In a second phase, IADB will make available another USD 56 million to purchase the loans from the SPV, aggregate them and issue them as green bonds on the Mexican market. The Clean Technology Fund makes available another USD 19 million as a credit guarantee for the underlying loans. Additional support is provided through non-reimbursable technical co-operation to develop capacity and knowledge for the assessment and identification of energy efficiency opportunities in accordance to the guidelines for energy efficiency projects. The project is now being replicated across Latin America with funding that has been made available by the Green Climate Fund (GCF) in November 2015.

Source : European Commission (2016), *Study on the potential for green bond finance for resource-efficient investments,* Publications Office of the European Union, Luxembourg. http://ec.europa.eu/environment/enveco/pdf/potential-green-bond.pdf.

Green bonds

Green bonds have rapidly become an important source of finance for projects in the green economy, including low carbon and climate resilient infrastructure and green business investments. In 2016, USD 95 billion worth of green bonds were issued, a sharp increase from USD 3 billion in 2011 (OECD 2017). While green bonds are a valuable tool for supporting access to sustainable finance, "bonds typically have to have a size of above USD 200 million to be relevant for institutional investors" (European Commission 2016). To address the fact that SMEs generally seek significantly lower sums than this, IFIs are developing green bonds targeted at supporting SMEs by aggregating and securitising loans for SMEs, and then issuing the resulting green bonds to investors. This helps bring in investors into markets which they might otherwise view as being less financially developed, as it provides investors some assurance through institutional involvement. It also decouples green loans from local interest rates, and allows for longer payback periods, depending on the specifics of the bond being issued.

Asset based financing

In OECD countries and increasingly in emerging economies, asset-based finance is used by SMEs for their working capital needs and to support domestic and international trade. Through asset-based finance, firms obtain funding based on the value of specific assets, including accounts receivables, inventory, machinery, equipment and real estate, rather than on their own credit standing. In this way, it can serve the needs of young and small firms that have difficulties in accessing traditional lending (OECD 2015b). To support access to green finance, institutions can create special funds dedicated to providing asset-based finance specifically to designated green assets.

Policies to promote asset-based finance relate primarily to the regulatory framework, which is key to enable the use of a broad set of assets to secure loans. Across OECD countries, active policies exist to support asset-based finance for businesses that are unable to meet credit standards associated with long-term credit (OECD 2015b).

One example of asset based financing is warehouse receipt financing (WRF). In WRF, farmers, food processors, or exporters place their goods in a secure warehouse owned by a third party. They are issued a receipt for the goods, which can then be used as collateral for getting a loan from a financial institution. Depending on the structure of the WRF arrangement, once the goods are sold to a buyer, the buyer can either pay the borrower or pay the funds directly to the financial institution. Enabling factors for WRF include supporting legislation, a responsible regulatory agency, licensed and supervised public warehouses, and banks familiar with warehouse receipts (Hollinger et al. 2015).

Microfinance

The money required for efficiency investments, especially for microenterprises, is often more than what is on hand as cashflow but less than what traditional banks offer as loans. Microfinance institutions are already active in the EaP countries – in 2012, there were 12 in Armenia, 30 in Azerbaijan, and 60 each in Georgia and Moldova. Microfinance institutions are often familiar with the communities they serve and can help reach microenterprises that would otherwise to access finance (OECD 2016). These microloans can make a major difference in microenterprises' ability to pursue efficiency gains, such as better equipment or structural changes that support better energy use and bottom-line savings on energy purchases. They can also act as conduits to help develop the understanding of microenterprises in terms of the costs and potential benefits of investing in more efficient equipment for their businesses. This can be as simple as more efficient refrigeration equipment for a food processor, or more energy efficient heating systems. However, for larger investments, such as more efficient production machinery or rooftop solar installations, the interest rates offered by MFIs may be too high.

In Tajikistan, the Asian Development Bank's Access to Green Finance Project provides 8.8 million USD for five year local currency dominated credit lines for selected microfinance institutions. The loans support microenterprises and households in making investments in more energy efficient and environmental friendly approaches, and have a maximum value of 5 000 USD. The government of Japan is providing additional support (750 000 USD) for technical assistance training to the microfinance institutions involved, with a particular focus on building capacity of the institutions around green finance and investments in efficiency (OECD 2016).

Conclusion

This toolkit chapter is a brief overview of what is a complex challenge for countries around the world. There is no one silver-bullet solution though, and the recommendations presented here act in concert to support access to finance for green SMEs of all types. SMEs are incredibly heterogeneous as a group, spanning every sector of the economy and ranging in size from a handful of employees to hundreds, and from cutting edge start-ups driving innovation in new green technology to local grocery stores that could save on their energy bill by investing in more efficient fridges. Meeting the needs of diverse SMEs requires a broad array of different solutions working in concert, and a co-ordinated policy response.

Recommendations

- Governments can support SMEs in accessing finance by raising awareness of the options that are available to them, and building the capacity of SMEs to assess the attractiveness of different finance options for their particular circumstances. SMEs should also be supported in building their capacity to better make the case to lending institutions of what their business fundamentals are and what the benefits to their business are going to be if they are able to invest in greener practices.
- Financial institutions should also be supported in building capacity so that they can better conduct due diligence and assess the risk factors of supporting green SMEs, and thus better assign interest rates and collateral requirements. Governments can also raise awareness among smaller financial institutions that are used by SMEs of available options for funds they can take part in to support green SMEs.
- Supporting soft loans or interest rate subsidies for green SMEs to encourage access to bank finance should be explored with a critical eye. While potentially beneficial for increasing green SME access to finance, there is a hazard of lending institutions keeping interest rates high if there is no impetus to lower them due to the expectation of subsidisation.
- In addition to making it easier to access existing bank finance, governments should support the development of non-bank financial channels for SMEs. This potentially decouples the availability of finance from interest rates and collateral requirements. Green bonds that aggregate and securitise loans into packages which can then be floated for investment can provide an important source of non-bank finance for SMEs. Asset-based financing is also an important form of non-bank finance.

References

EC (2016), *Study on the potential for green bond finance for resource-efficient investments*, Publications Office of the European Union, Luxembourg, http://ec.europa.eu/environment/enveco/pdf/potential-green-bond.pdf.

EC (2007), *Small, clean and competitive: A programme to help small and medium-sized enterprises comply with environmental legislation*, Case studies and good practices in environmental compliance assistance, Commission staff working document, European Commission, Brussels, 8.10.2007.

EC (2004), Annex to the *Report from the Commission to the Council and the European Parliament on Incentives for EMAS Registered Organisations*, Commission Staff Working Document, European Commission, Brussels, http://ec.europa.eu/transparency/regdoc/rep/1/2004/EN/1-2004-745-EN-F1-1.Pdf.

ECOS (2012), *2012 State Innovations*, Environmental Council of the States, https://www.ecos.org/documents/2012-state-innovations/.

EU (2017), *Identification and promotion of energy efficiency investments*, EU Neighbours east, www.euneighbours.eu/en/east/eu-in-action/projects/identification-and-promotion-energy-efficiency-investments.

Hollinger, F; L. Rutten and K. Kiriakov (2015), *The use of warehouse receipt finance in transition countries*, Working paper, FAO Investment Centre, World Bank Group, https://www.agrifinfacility.org/sites/agrifin/files/TechSum6_UseOfWarehouseReceipt_1520066_Web.pdf.

OECD (2017), *Mobilising Bond Markets for a Low-Carbon Transition*, Green Finance and Investment, OECD Publishing, Paris, http://dx.doi.org/10.1787/9789264272323-en.

OECD (2017-forthcoming), *Mobilising Finance for Climate Action in Georgia*, OECD Publishing, Paris, www.oecd.org/env/outreach/eap-tf.htm.

OECD (2016a), *Environmental Lending in EU Eastern Partnership Countries*, Green Finance and Investment, OECD Publishing, Paris, France, http://dx.doi.org/10.1787/9789264252189-en.

OECD (2016b), *Financing Climate Action in Eastern Europe, the Caucasus and Central Asia*, Green Finance and Investment, OECD Publishing, Paris, http://dx.doi.org/10.1787/9789264266339-en.

OECD (2015a), *Promoting better environmental performance of small and medium-sized enterprises in Armenia*, Pilot project report, Greening Economies in the Eastern Neighbourhood programme, Organisation for Economic Co-operation and Development, Paris, www.oecd.org/environment/outreach/SME-greening-country-pilot-report-Armenia-en.pdf.

OECD (2015b), *New Approaches to SME and Entrepreneurship Financing: Broadening the Range of Instruments*, OECD Centre for Entrepreneurship, SMEs and Local Development, OECD Publishing, Paris, France, https://www.oecd.org/cfe/smes/New-Approaches-SME-full-report.pdf.

Part II

Guidance for issue-specific implementation in pilot countries

Chapter 8

Simplified Environmental Management Systems for SMEs in Armenia

This chapter explores simplified Environmental Management Systems (EMS) in detail, and develops the concept for a proposed simplified EMS for Armenia. The chapter begins with the experiences and approaches of different EU countries in using simplified EMS. This is used as a springboard to build up the proposal for Armenia. For the simplified EMS, detailed step-by-step instructions are included for each level, accompanied by illustrative examples from EU countries. While the EMS was developed for Armenia at the behest of the stakeholder, the guidance is potentially applicable to other EAP countries.

Simplified Environmental Management Systems

Recently, many OECD countries have started to put an emphasis on policy instruments that promote green behaviour of enterprises, including the establishment of Environmental Management Systems (EMSs). However, the organisational complexity of internationally recognised EMS standards (ISO 14001 and the European Eco-Management and Audit Scheme, EMAS) makes it difficult for SMEs, with their human and financial resource constraints, to adopt and get certified to these standards. In a number of European countries, business associations have designed simplified environmental management schemes that allow SMEs to get recognition for less ambitious but still valuable improvements in their environmental management, and, if they wish, eventually qualify for full certification to an international EMS standard. The examples of such schemes include EcoMerit (Ireland), Green Ticks (Scotland), 1.2.3. Environnement and EnVol (France) and Programa e+5 (Spain).

Generally, a simplified EMS comprises several steps/levels that allow an enterprise to get recognition for attaining the corresponding requirements. The Scottish Green Ticks and the Spanish Programa e+5 are based on British Standard BS 8555. In Scotland, the Green Ticks comprise five levels, and the company is awarded one additional "tick" for reaching each of them. Usually, there is a possibility of achieving full ISO 14001 or EMAS certification at the final level of certification, for those enterprise that wish to comply with international standards. This gradual approach allows SMEs to choose the level of an EMS that they desire or are able to obtain while still leaving room for improvements in the future. The French 1.2.3. Environnement has only three levels of requirements. A simpler approach is likely to be better suited to the needs of SMEs. Enterprises are encouraged to use the labels of the EMS certification on their marketing materials to distinguish themselves as "green" businesses.

Simplified EMS schemes are usually run and promoted by business groups or associations, sometimes with financial support from the government. Such approach facilitates EMS implementation and ensures information sharing (especially regarding legal requirements) between enterprises, business organisations and governments. The actual auditing is usually carried out by accredited private companies.

These companies set a specific fee for EMS certification services. They provide SMEs with annual verification audits, training and on-going assistance at each level of EMS implementation (Box 8.3). The fees are established at rates affordable for SMEs while taking into account the costs for the certification body, the size of an enterprise and the EMS implementation level. Audit and certification fees could be supported by grants provided by national or local governments.

In general, an internal and an external audit are required to verify the attainment of each level of certification. In an internal audit, an enterprise should analyse and make available the information on its waste energy and water consumption, as well as on its management procedures. An external audit should be conducted by an accredited certification company or an EMS-scheme implementing organisation or business association to verify the attainment of a certain level of an EMS.

Box 8.1. **EcoMerit scheme, Ireland**

Econcertive is an independent company established in 2009 which provides environmental support to SMEs and larger businesses. Econcertive has designed, owns and operates the EcoMerit scheme, supported by funds of contributor organisations and client fees. In addition, it is supported and monitored by the Environmental Protection Agency (EPA) and local councils. Its approach concentrates on cost savings and performance improvement rather than compliance.

Enterprises that want to apply for EcoMerit certification need to pay a Review and Certification fee during the first year of application (varies from EUR 200 to EUR 800, depending on the size of the enterprise); with subsequent fees paid during the second and third years of surveillance and support (varies from EUR 125 to EUR 350). These fees cover the following services provided by the certifying body: monitoring support; on-site review visit and follow-up support visit; assistance in developing environmental policy, monitoring and improvements; on-going telephone support; a final evaluation visit three months after application; and EcoMerit certification. If the target cost savings are not reached, the fees could be refunded by Econcertive. The fees can also be subsidised by the government: in 2012, the Irish EPA launched a grant scheme to support enterprises that wish to implement green practices.

By 2012, EcoMerit scheme was awarded to 65 companies, which are also listed on the Econcertive website. On average, these companies have reduced their costs on energy, waste and water bills by EUR 5 774 annually (between 2009 and 2012).

The general requirements for achieving EcoMerit are the same as for any recognised EMS scheme:

- an environmental policy
- a commitment to pollution prevention
- an improvement plan
- performance monitoring.

An Econcertive-assigned advisor helps the applying enterprise to prepare the EcoMerit scheme implementation and improvement plan tailored to the specific needs of the enterprise (usually, a number of options is suggested, for an enterprise to choose the most suitable one). Thus, there is no need for an enterprise to hire a consultant.

Source : EcoMerit (2015), *Environmental Business Support*, www.ecocert.ie.

A proposed simplified EMS scheme for Armenia

In Armenia, a simplified EMS scheme could be administered by a business association (e.g. the Republican Union of Employers or the Chamber of Commerce and Industry) with support from the SME DNC. The scheme would rely on private consultants accredited to conduct verification audits under the ISO 14000 series standards, but the business association would issue appropriate certificates.

Based on the experience of several OECD countries' EMS programmes, the following three certification levels are recommended, where each level corresponds to an operational EMS.

Level 1: Established baseline and environmental policy, applicable requirements identified

The first level ensures the commitment of the company's management and the identification of environmental objectives and business opportunities related to them. It is important that all employees in a small enterprise and all management levels in medium-sized business participate in this process. Simultaneously, Level 1 EMS serves to identify legal requirements along with relevant industry sector norms. It also helps to set up control measures and mechanisms to ensure compliance with them. Business associations or specialised agencies can help SMEs by providing technical assistance in defining the scope of specific regulatory requirements.

This level plays a crucial role in the initial setup of the environmental vector for an SME. It defines a framework for environmental action, together with the sensitive issues an enterprise will need to address (e.g. waste management, emissions to air, use of raw materials and natural resources, etc.). Knowledge platforms inclusive of the information on required and possible environmental actions and respective regulations in a given industry sector can facilitate this initial setup and help to channel the management commitment. In the experience of the EU countries (Boxes 8.1, 8.3, 8.4 and 8.5), continuous training and awareness raising campaigns are provided to SMEs by business organisations and specialised NGOs.

Steps to attain Level 1

1. Ensure a ***management commitment*** at a high corporate level towards ambitious environmental goals. Such environmental commitment should be associated with specific business drivers: cost savings, risk management, marketing opportunities, meeting demand from external parties, etc. It is also advisable to designate an EMS implementation team or a responsible person in order to follow through on this commitment.
2. Take stock of a history of the company's environment-related activities and related challenges as a background for a ***baseline assessment***. Conduct a clear yet simple assessment of the "big picture" (a more detailed assessment of environmental impacts would take place in further EMS implementation phases). At this stage, it is important to identify the environmental impacts of the key activities, products and services of the enterprise. Again, it is preferable to single out "quick wins" in terms of cost savings that would be generated by addressing these impacts.
3. Once the baseline assessment is complete, develop a ***draft environmental policy*** for the enterprise. If an environmental policy is already in place, it should be tailored according to the baseline assessment and current needs of the enterprise. The environmental policy can be altered at the higher levels of EMS implementation.
4. Identify ***applicable environmental legal requirements*** for the given activity. The existing legislation at the national and local levels with regard to the enterprise's activities should be verified.
5. Identify ***other environmental norms*** applicable to the business: codes of practice, industry standards, voluntary agreements, internal management requirements, and contractual requirements.
6. ***Structure*** all the applicable requirements by type of the enterprise's activity.

7. ***Analyse the actual level of compliance*** in order to determine the areas of non-compliance and ensure further effective compliance monitoring within the enterprise.
8. Design ***operational control procedures*** to tackle possible cases of non-compliance and strengthen compliance monitoring. Well-designed control procedures will simplify the EMS implementation if the enterprise wishes to go further in the process.

Box 8.2. **Designing an environmental policy**

Environmental policy is a public statement that defines the commitment and future actions of the enterprise to pursue environmental goals. Typically, it should not exceed one A4 page in order to keep it simple and concise.

An environmental policy should include a description of the nature and scale of the enterprise (scope of an EMS), a list of broad environmental commitments and intentions, and an outline of the main activities, products or services that will be covered by an EMS.

Recommendations:

- At the level 1 the environmental policy should be kept general, in order to avoid frequent alterations.
- Vague terms, such as "environmentally friendly" should be avoided, as they are hard to define.
- The policy should be relevant to the nature of an enterprise and its industry sector.

Source : IEMA (2015), *BS 8555 SME Workbook*, http://ems.iema.net/acorn_scheme/bs8555/phase1.

Box 8.3. **Simplified EMS in France: 1.2.3. Environnement**

1.2.3. Environnement provides SMEs with a possibility to acquire three levels of an EMS. The French Chambers of Commerce and Industry (CCI France) in partnership with several French companies and public organisations, and supported by the country's environment ministry and the Environmental Agency (ADEME), use 1.2.3 Environnement to assist enterprises in implementing an EMS. Similarly to other simplified EMSs, this scheme allows an enterprise to choose to comply with a level it desires.

415 companies have been involved in the implementation of 1.2.3 Environnement since 2007. The regional Chambers of Commerce and Industry provide a consultant dedicated to helping SMEs in the establishment of a 1.2.3 Environnement scheme. Additionally, business associations and NGOs are helping the enterprise throughout the process. At least seven companies in France, accredited by CCI France, are offering this certification. The applying enterprises are certified with one of the three levels after an external audit by one of these certification bodies is conducted. The certification is valid for a three-year period with an annual verification audit.

Requirements:

- *Level 1 Environnement (levels 1 and 2 of BS 8555)* – Formalise an EMS – the enterprise must conduct an initial environmental review, ensure a commitment of the top management, establish an action plan, identify the most significant environmental impacts and comply with legal obligations. At this level the knowledge of the required environmental principles is guaranteed, as well as the identification of environmental priorities of an enterprise, translated into a coherent action plan.

Box 8.3. **Simplified EMS in France: 1.2.3. Environnement** *(continued)*

- *Level 2 Environnement (levels 3 of BS 8555)* – Establish an environmental programme – the enterprise must develop an environmental management programme that is continuously reviewed and improved, anticipate risks and emergency preparedness plan, and ensure continuous trainings and awareness raising. This level enables an enterprise to improve and structure its environmental action plan, prioritise the activities and establish an environmental management programme well-adapted to its industry sector.
- *Level 3 Environnement (levels 4, 5 and 6 of BS 8555)* – Identify priority actions and conduct an audit – the enterprise must conduct regular internal audits and management review, ensure documentation of planning and design operation controls, checking, monitoring and corrective actions, establish external and internal communications, and define roles and responsibilities within the enterprise. Compliance with the requirements of the third level ensures an establishment of a full EMS.

Source : French Chambers of Commerce and Industry (2015), www.cci.fr/web/123environnement.

Box 8.4. **The Green Ticks scheme in Scotland**

Green Ticks is a tool to develop an EMS according to the national BS 8555 standard while getting certified with an additional "tick" for each level. The certification is provided by the Bright Green Business organisation. The organisation supports an enterprise through implementation, inspection and maintenance of the EMS. By doing so, it helps to reduce costs, boost competitiveness, enhance customers' perceptions and meet supply chain obligations. This scheme was designed specifically for Scottish businesses but is recognised in the rest of the UK and in Ireland.

A consultant-advisor is provided to an enterprise in order to help it define a desirable level and required internal and external documentation. An enterprise that complies with all the requirements of a specific level, receives an inspection report and a certificate of compliance. Additionally, it will be listed on the official Green Ticks website. Re-inspection is conducted on an annual basis.

EMS requirements (BS 8555 based) are divided into six different levels, with the last one corresponding to accredited EMAS and/or ISO 14001:

- *Level 1*: Management commitment and establishment of a baseline and environmental policy
- *Level 2*: Identifying and ensuring compliance with legal and other requirements
- *Level 3*: Developing objectives, targets and programmes
- *Level 4*: Implementation and operation of the EMS
- *Level 5*: Checking, audit and review
- *Level 6*: EMS acknowledgment (EMAS or ISO 14001).

Sources: Bright Green Business (2015), www.brightgreenbusiness.org.uk ; Green Ticks (2015), greenticks.org.uk.

Box 8.5. Programa e+5 in Spain

Programa e+5 was introduced in 1999 and was developed by Fundacion Entorno (non-profit organisation promoting sustainable development in Spanish companies) with support from the Spanish Ministry of Science and Technology. It is based on the British *BS 8555* standard, with an inclusion of preliminary review of legal requirements at Level 1 (e+1).

Its two main objectives are:

- To support enterprises in the gradual implementation of an EMS that improves environmental performance and satisfies the demand from customers without implementation of a full ISO 14001 or EMAS scheme; and
- To provide an enterprise with a tool to evaluate the environmental performance of its supply chain.

As every certification level (e+1 – e+5), an enterprise gains recognition for its achievements. The programme provides local consultants to assist enterprises throughout the EMS implementation process. Face-to-face training sessions, distance learning and specific materials dissemination are also part of the programme. Additionally, a number of trainings are provided for internal auditors.

So far, more than 900 companies have joined the programme, among those over 230 already benefit from the competitive improvements of the environmental qualification.

Source : Observatorio Ambiental y de Responsabilidad Social en el Ámbito Sanitario (2014), www.observatorioambiental.net/es/lineas-de-estudio/programa-e-5.

Level 2: Established objectives, targets and programmes

At Level 2, the enterprise is expected to establish the substance of a functional EMS and provide a more specific framework for further development. This phase concentrates on management mechanisms behind the EMS and environmental programme of the enterprise.

Built on the results of the first level, an enterprise will now be able to evaluate the significance of its environmental policy and make necessary improvements. A coherent environmental management programme and performance monitoring will allow more cost savings and enhanced environmental performance. The EMS certification body should provide training programmes to maximise the efficiency of the enterprise's environmental programme.

Steps to attain Level 2

1. ***Evaluate the aspects and impacts*** identified as part of the baseline assessment at Level 1. A uniform sector-specific approach could be useful in doing this.
2. Include those aspects that appear to be significant for the enterprise in an updated and ***more specific environmental policy***.
3. Develop clear ***objectives and targets for environmental performance*** improvement in accordance with the significant aspects and impacts.
4. Develop ***environmental performance indicators*** that will help monitoring improvement towards the defined targets and objectives.

5. Define more specific ***environmental management programmes*** within the company: designate responsibilities, timescales and necessary resources, as well as an operational control procedure.
6. Put in place ***a training programme*** associated with environmental management programme activities. The certification body could provide support with training implementation.

Level 3: Established EMS documentation, monitoring and audit procedures

The third level provides for the formalisation of all documentation developed at Levels 1 and 2. The enterprise should be able to implement and operate the full EMS, with continuous audit and operation and documentation controls in place. The visibility of environmental certification should be ensured through external communication channels.

Steps to attain Level 3

1. Finalise the enterprise's ***environmental management structure*** and define the respective responsibilities within the enterprise.
2. Establish and maintain clear ***communication practices***. Particular attention should be paid to internal communication channels, i.e. to the integration of employees into the system.
3. Make sure all the ***documentation, control and record-keeping*** systems are in place.
4. Establish internal EMS ***audit procedures*** and related competences.
5. Management of the enterprise should ***review and communicate audit findings*** to other people in the enterprise.
6. Ensure continuous ***improvement of the environmental performance*** and sustainability of the EMS of the enterprise through periodic management reviews.

Conclusion

EMS systems such as ISO 14001 are often too complex and costly to achieve for SMEs. A simplified EMS offers a feasible solution for SMEs that are willing to improve their environmental performance. This approach can be tailored to specific needs of an SME while taking into account other factors the enterprise needs to cope with in their day-to-day activities. Experiences in other countries have shown that for a simplified system to succeed in Armenia, it should have graduated levels that can be progressively achieved, to encourage both performance as well as accessibility. It should also be developed in co-operation with trade organisations and local authorities, to ensure that it is structured in a way that makes sense to SMEs, that different levels of government have expertise to support it, and that SMEs in different sectors are aware of the simplified EMS' existence and have an understanding of how they can achieve different levels.

References

Observatorio Ambiental y de Responsabilidad Social en el Ámbito Sanitario (2014), *Programa e+5*, www.observatorioambiental.net/es/lineas-de-estudio/programa-e-5.

Bright Green Business (2015), www.brightgreenbusiness.org.uk;.

Green Ticks (2015), greenticks.org.uk.

French Chambers of Commerce and Industry (2015), *1.2.3.Environnement*, www.cci.fr/web/123environnement.

IEMA (2015), *BS 8555 SME Workbook*, Institute of Environmental Management & Assessment, http://ems.iema.net/acorn_scheme/bs8555/phase1.

EcoMerit (2015), *Environmental Business Support*, www.ecocert.ie.

Chapter 9

Information scheme for greening SMEs in the Republic of Moldova

This chapter lays out a proposed Information Scheme for greening SMEs in the Republic of Moldova. The proposed information scheme includes five different information based tools. Each tool is introduced with relevant objectives, timeframes, links to other instruments, target audience, and proposed implementing partners highlighted. These tools include a subscription-based "Regulatory Watch" service; direct capacity building and awareness raising events, publications, web-tools, and face-to-face advice. The chapter clarifies the roles of different state and non-state actors, and provides suggestions for a broad performance evaluation approach for the proposed Information Scheme.

Introduction

As explored in Chapter 4 of this toolkit, successful communication is a vital part of supporting the uptake of green SME policies. The strategy developed in this chapter is an Information Scheme to raise awareness among Moldovan SMEs on good environmental management practices and the potential performance and efficiency benefits. It is crucial to emphasise that green practices present SMEs with business opportunities and innovative ways of solving financial constraints of business development. In order for this Strategy to be effective, it should be based on the following principles:

- *Clarity*: Transmitted messages via each information-based tool should be clear, concise and differentiated while targeting different SMEs activity sectors. The roles of institutions and their responsibilities should be defined clearly.
- *Simplicity*: Institutions need to translate complicated terminology they use into simple messages and step-by-step guidance for SMEs.
- *Coherence*: All the information-based tools should be systematic, with uniform mechanism behind them.
- *Co-operation*: Institutions will ensure the success of the strategy if they work together to promote the information-based tools in a transparent manner.

Information-based instruments

This Information Scheme proposes five types of information-based tools for implementation in the Republic of Moldova: "regulatory watch", direct capacity building and awareness raising events, publications, web-tools, and face-to-face advice. The effectiveness of each tool is increased when combined with others.

The Ministries of Economy, Environment and Agriculture, ODIMM, Chamber of Commerce and Industry, Energy Efficiency Agency, Cleaner production centres, sectoral business associations and local authorities are the key institutions for this Information Scheme. The Ministry of Economy will co-ordinate the work of other implementing institutions.

Regulatory watch

Implementing partners: The Chamber of Commerce and Industry of the Republic of Moldova will play the leading role in "regulatory watch" development, to be supported by the Ministry of Environment (general environmental regulation) and the Ministry of Agriculture (environmental regulation in agricultural sector). CCI RM should gather and sort the information prepared by other partners. ODIMM and sectoral business associations could contribute by advising on the website/newsletter structure in order to make sure that it is tailored to the needs of SMEs.

Objectives: This subscription-based service is an easy and effective way to convey the message to SMEs on relevant legislative developments as well as upcoming applicable amendments to regulation. Regulatory watch can take a form of either e-mail or mobile regular updates.

Target audience: SMEs in all sectors.

Key message: In the form of an electronic newsletter (e-mail or mobile) keep the subscribers updated on current and forthcoming environmental regulation. However, this instrument's outreach is limited by accessibility to internet.

Process description: "Regulatory watch" subscription service on regulatory information is a web-based tool, where SMEs are able to choose the regulatory information applicable to their particular type of business. The core practical information on the following topics could be made available at the website of **the CCI RM**: environmental medium-specific and cross-media regulation, applicable taxes and fees, and recent environmental policies. Additional industry-sector and case-specific information, such as personalised guidance (based on the topics, industries or key words indicated during the subscription process) will be sent in a regular newsletter either monthly or quarterly. Subscribers could also indicate their newsletter type preference (e-mail or phone). **The Ministries of Environment and Agriculture** will help with content development in their respective fields. **ODIMM and business associations** will assist the CCI RM in developing a targeted and concise website and newsletter structure by analysing the content prepared by the governmental institutions and providing feedback, while keeping in mind the needs of SMEs.

Timeframe: The website development and newsletter establishment should take from 6 to 12 months. Right after the launch it is strongly recommended that the first 6 months will be a trial no-fee period for subscribers.

Links to other instruments: The CCI RM can also provide an option of a printed newsletter for SMEs in rural areas with limited access to the internet. This could be a short-term option advertised through local community events organised by **local authorities in collaboration with business associations**.

Direct capacity building and awareness raising: workshops, seminars, trainings and community events

Implementing partners: ODIMM should be the lead organisation in direct capacity building and awareness raising of SMEs. Energy Efficiency Agency and cleaner production centres will organise workshops on their respective topics. Business associations and local governments will hold local capacity building and community events. The national government will provide partial financial support for the organisation of relevant workshops, seminars and training events.

Objectives: Direct capacity building seminars, workshops and trainings, and community events help to bridge the gap between theoretical knowledge received from other sources (e.g. publications, websites, newsletters) and specific SME business cases (by industry sector, size and specialisation). The constructive knowledge obtained from such events provides better understanding of environmental practices' implications for particular businesses. It also gives an opportunity for local outreach in the regions, which is especially important for business with no or limited access to the internet.

Target audience: Two types of capacity building events should be distinguished: those targeting SMEs in specific industry sectors and those for trainers and/or assistance providers.

Key message: Training SME managers on how to integrate good environmental behaviour into business practices and on the basics of environmental management. Additionally, SMEs will be provided with information on such cleaner technologies, resource and energy efficient practices, and their cost saving potential. The trainers and assistance providers will learn the key issues and techniques that SMEs of the relevant sector should be aware of and incorporate into their business planning.

Process description: "Train-the-trainer" workshops could be directed at company managers and experts that are members of local business associations. Such events will be supported by **the Ministry of Environment** in collaboration with the **Ministries of Economy and Agriculture** when applicable. As the end result, environmental management should become a mainstream element in the business strategy. **CCI RM** should also contribute to such training events through the existing industry fairs and exhibitions, where they can introduce new technological advancements that will be helpful for the greening of SMEs. This instrument can also be used as direct capacity building for SMEs; however, it is suitable only for medium-sized and sometimes small enterprises, which can afford to send an environmental manager or another representative to such an event. **Cleaner production centres** can provide training for trainers (business associations' representatives, preferably environmental managers) through the National Cleaner Production Programme.

As the lead organisation, **ODIMM** should be responsible for holding regional and national level workshops, seminars, trainings and round tables in the framework of its "Efficient management of business" educational module with a focus on greening SMEs. ODIMM can also provide trainings on green innovation and efficiency of environmental management, where SMEs will be able to share their experience and learn new business practices. ODIMM will likewise use its capacity by creating and chairing an annual knowledge sharing platform, where SMEs would have an opportunity to learn from larger companies' environmental best practices. **CCI RM** and ODIMM may want to hold industry sector-specific events at the regional level in order to promote relevant green practices. Business associations (sector-based) are encouraged to collaborate in organisation of, or participate in, local capacity building events.

The **Energy Efficiency Agency** could organise seminars, conferences or exhibitions tailored to the needs and capacities of SMEs to promote energy efficiency measures and renewable energy sources. The optimisation of energy consumption presents an important costs savings opportunity for SMEs. Furthermore, during awareness raising and capacity building events SMEs may learn about funding possibilities offered by the Energy Efficiency Fund.

Similarly to the Energy Efficiency Agency, the **cleaner production centres** will tailor their capacity building events to the needs of SMEs. They need to formulate a clear message with supporting cases from local practice on business advantages of cleaner production and resource efficiency practices and deliver it at their training events and seminars.

Local authorities and business associations should ensure the regional outreach of the capacity building and awareness raising events to SMEs in rural areas.

Timeframe: In the short term, for the period of two to four years, capacity building events should be conducted more intensively, especially at the local level. Workshops and seminars will be conducted whenever relevant in the long term. Local community events will be held on a bi-annual basis during the first two years and thereafter on an annual basis.

Links to other instruments: This instrument is highly interlinked with other information-based tools. It presents an opportunity to disseminate information on available and forthcoming publications, as well as web-based tools. Communities with low or no access to the internet will have opportunities to learn about the "regulatory watch" led by CCI RM and the Advisory website developed by the Ministry of Environment.

Publications (compliance guidance, best practice guidance/case studies, methodological materials, industrial journals, print newsletters, policy highlights, policy manuals)

Implementing partners: The Ministries of Economy, Environment and Agriculture will provide their inputs on compliance guidelines, their respective policy updates through policy highlights and manuals, as well as final products of projects conducted jointly with international organisations, NGOs and academic institutions. Cleaner production centres, the Energy Efficiency Agency, ODIMM and the Chamber of Commerce and Industry will disseminate information in their respective fields by creating best practice guidance and compiling case studies of business success stories, preparing methodological materials, industrial magazines and print newsletters, with ODIMM as the project leader.

Objectives: Printed materials are of high importance for regional SMEs that do not have access to the internet. This instrument also helps communicating and explaining to SMEs the existing policies for the support of green practices. "Pocket guides" (succinct "how to" brochures on green practices for specific activity sectors) will promote business opportunities (enhanced performance and cost savings) generated by green practices.

Target audience: SMEs in all sectors, civil society, business associations.

Key message: Best practice guidance and methodological guides will illustrate the "business benefits first" approach explaining how to turn environmental challenges into business opportunities. This includes conveying the information on how to reduce costs through energy and resource efficiency along with using cleaner production practices.

Process description: **The Ministry of Economy** will provide its policy documents on the green economy with their implications for green transformation of SMEs in all industry sectors. The Ministry should highlight new business opportunities (including cost savings) created by green economy policies.

The **Ministry of Environment** will develop general and industry sector-specific compliance guidance documents, whereas the **Ministry of Agriculture** and the **Energy Efficiency Agency** will prepare guidance for the agricultural sector and cross-sectoral guidance on energy efficiency, respectively. The guidance documents should distinguish between mandatory elements of compliance with the law and recommended green practices beneficial for business performance. Furthermore, the **Energy Efficiency Agency** and **cleaner production centres** should issue technical reports and methodological guides explaining to SMEs how small business can follow such practices.

CCI RM should produce the print equivalent of the "regulatory watch" newsletter for SMEs with limited or no access to internet, or those that prefer print materials.

Jointly with other institutions, **ODIMM** should establish the framework for environmental industry magazines and brief "pocket guides" on green practices. Industry magazines could be issued on a quarterly or bi-annual basis. They may cover topics on air quality, conservation, energy, food and packaging, land management, sustainable construction works, transport and waste and recycling, etc. Short business stories will highlight the most innovative, performant and efficient green business in each industry. Support organisations should provide their respective inputs to ODIMM, with CCI RM contributing the most.

Local authorities should select publications relevant to the business activity of their regions and ensure the dissemination of these materials to local SMEs.

Timeframe: Guidance materials will be prepared in the course of the first two years, with regular updates to be made in the longer time perspective. Case studies are an effective practice for keeping SMEs informed in the short term (up to five years), but their relevance will diminish in the long term. Industrial magazines and newsletters should be distributed on an annual or bi-annual basis (in some cases newsletters can be distributed on a quarterly basis, if there is a need for more frequent updates). Other publications will be prepared for dissemination upon availability.

Links to other instruments: Print material is a valuable instrument in the short term. This tool will help address the outreach issue for the "regulatory watch" newsletter and promote the web based tools and capacity building events at the initial phase of the Strategy.

Web-based tools (compliance guidance and green practices website)

Implementing partners: The Ministry of Environment should be the leading institution for the website working group. The Ministries of Economy and Agriculture, the Energy Efficiency Agency, cleaner production centres, CCI RM, ODIMM and business associations will participate in the working group for the website content development.

Objectives: A government-sponsored environmental guidance website will serve as an assistance tool created particularly for SMEs.

Target audience: SMEs in all sectors, business associations and civil society.

Key message: As a joint initiative of the government, CCI RM and several business associations, the website will cover two types of information: guidance on environmental compliance and good practices adapted to each industry sector.

Process description: The website could be developed in two ways. The **Ministry of Environment** can re-design its webpage for hosting environmental guidance tailored for SMEs. As an alternative, a specialised site on sector-specific green practices could be co-founded by the government (including **ODIMM**), **CCI RM** and several **business associations**. In the latter case, Moldova's Official Business Portal could serve as a platform to host such website.

The website will be linked to relevant government websites, as well as to websites of the partner organisations in the **working group**, so that the compliance information is made available. The working group will put its efforts and resources in populating the website contents, covering a wide range of environmental topics. In addition, such website will feature factsheets on best environmental management practice in at least six industry-sectors, contacts database for advisory service providers, information on upcoming events for direct capacity building and awareness raising tools, and other relevant information. Further in the process of the website development, such features as interactive learning modules, self-assessment questionnaires and other tools could be added.

Timeframe: The website should be developed and populated with the core information in the course of the first two years. Additional features will appear progressively in the medium term (up to five years). Information will be updated continuously in the long term (over five years).

Links to other instruments: The website will have links to methodological materials, policy updates, "pocket guides", recent and upcoming capacity building and awareness raising events and other relevant products of this Scheme. Additionally, compliance guidance and green practices website could host the "regulatory watch" subscription service. In this case, the Ministry of Environment would play a leading role in implementing both instruments, which could also save costs for the internet-based tools development.

Advice (face-to-face)

Implementing partners: The Ministry of Environment, cleaner production centres, ODIMM.

Objectives: Similarly to other direct capacity building tools, face-to-face advice helps to bridge the gap between theoretical knowledge obtained via other information instruments and their practical implication.

Target audience: SMEs in all sectors

Key message: Providing enterprise-specific advice on technical environmental aspects not covered by the general and sector-specific guidance to a particular enterprise. Even though most of the environmental issues would be covered by the general guidance, face-to-face advice will help to eliminate or prevent the misinterpretation and uncertainty.

Process description: Most frequently, face-to-face advice is provided through audits of different environmental management aspects. The **Ministry of Environment** can provide advice to SMEs during its environmental inspections, or by distinguishing between the compliance visits and the advice and guidance visits. In this case, the environmental inspector will also be the advisor, which is better perceived by the enterprises. (This, however, will require recognition by the Ministry of Environment that compliance promotion is an essential part of its mandate.)

The majority of SMEs cannot afford a dedicated environmental manager. **ODIMM,** in collaboration with **sectoral business associations** and **NGOs,** could provide an "ad hoc environmental manager" service through their business support instruments. Given the general lack of such experts in Moldova, ODIMM could prepare a contacts database of available experts, whereas the sectoral business associations and NGOs could provide trained experts. There could be a possibility of co-financing such an expert by ODIMM. The role of this manager will be to help an SME to deal with its environmental management issues with very limited on-site presence (one or two days per month).

Similarly, **cleaner production centres** could use their resource and energy efficiency audits to advise SMEs on green practice opportunities to improve their business performance.

Timeframe: The integration of advice into environmental inspectors' site visits should be done in the medium- to long-term perspective. An "ad hoc environmental manager" service could be introduced already in the short term. Resource efficiency and cleaner production audits will continue to play an important role in the short and medium term (up to five years), but the demand for them could be expected to decrease in the longer term if other instruments of this Scheme are implemented in an appropriate and timely manner.

Links to other instruments: Representatives of the sectoral business associations and possibly NGOs could participate in "train-the-trainer" events to become "ad hoc environmental managers" and provide help to SMEs with limited capacities to manage their environmental activities.

Performance evaluation of instruments

Performance evaluation of instruments included in this Information Scheme could consist of a combination of quantitative compliance assistance indicators and additional qualitative measures. Quantitative indicators may include:

- number of activities or services provided by an institution over a given period
- number of events and participants who attended them
- number of copies of printed materials disseminated, etc.

The data for qualitative evaluation of outcomes could be collected through assessment forms, such as targeted satisfaction questionnaires. They could be collected either online (for "regulatory watch" newsletter subscribers, possibly on a quarterly basis, or hosted on the environmental guidance website) or in print (during capacity building and awareness raising events, exhibitions and face-to-face advice). The questionnaires should also be differentiated depending on the target audience (SMEs, business associations, civil society).

Financing

This Information Scheme does not cover budget aspects of the implementation of various information-based tools. However, it is suggested that most activities be co-financed by governmental funds. Some funds could be raised through payments for provided services. For example, the costs of some activities, such as a "regulatory watch" subscription service, could be partially recovered through fees paid by subscribers.

An additional study to elaborate a detailed budget forecast for the short-term and long-term implementation periods could be conducted by the National Institute of Economic Research or another organisation.

Conclusion

A well planned and implemented information scheme will be vital to greening Moldova's SMEs. Although this plan is structured with Moldova's specific state and non-state actors, the principles are broadly applicable to other EaP countries, with modifications for their national specifics. A good information scheme is multidimensional, and integrates a wide range of stakeholders, including those in the private sector. This helps provide legitimacy and encourage the successful delivery of information, as well as providing a conduit for feedback and an accessible method for SMEs to seek further guidance more directly. To avoid confusion and duplication, however, it is vitally important that there be clearly defined overall co-ordinating body who can also signpost resources and other actors.

Table 9.1. **Role of institutions in implementing specific information-based instruments**

	Regulatory watch	Capacity building and awareness raising	Publications	Web-based tools (website)	Face-to-face advice
Ministry of Economy		"Train-the-trainer" events, co-organising or co-funding workshops/seminars	Green economy policy documents highlighting new business opportunities	Website contributor: member of the working group	
Ministry of Environment	Content contributor/ environmental regulation	"Train-the-trainer" events, co-organising or co-funding workshops/seminars	General and industry sector-specific compliance guidance documents	Leading role: environmental guidance website, supported by the working group	Environmental inspections/guidance visits
Ministry of Agriculture	Content contributor/ regulation in agricultural sector	"Train-the-trainer" events, co-organising or co-funding workshops/seminars	Guidance for the agricultural sector	Website contributor: member of the working group	
ODIMM	Advisor	Leading role in direct capacity building and awareness raising of SMEs	Leading role: industry magazines, "pocket guides" on green practices	Advisor	"Ad hoc environmental manager" database of experts
Chamber of Commerce and Industry	"Regulatory watch" would be hosted on the CCI website (leading role)	"Train-the-trainer" events, industry fairs and exhibitions	Print newsletters, magazines; assist ODIMM in "pocket guides" development	Website contributor: member of the working group	
Energy Efficiency Agency		Seminars, conferences or exhibitions to raise awareness and build capacity of SMEs	Cross-sectoral guidance on energy efficiency. Assist ODIMM in "pocket guides" development	Website contributor: member of the working group	
Cleaner production centres		"Train-the-trainer" events and seminars for SMEs	Technical reports and methodological guides; assist ODIMM in "pocket guides" development	Website contributor: member of the working group	Advice through resource and energy efficiency audits
Business associations (sectoral) and NGOs	Advisor representing SMEs	Regional outreach, community events		Advisor representing SMEs	"Ad hoc environmental manager" experts

Chapter 10

Guidance on environmental regulation of SMEs with a low level of environmental risk in Ukraine

This chapter provides guidance on how Ukraine can reform its environmental regulation of low-risk SMEs, and where possible move to a regulatory regime based on general binding rules (GBRs). The chapter begins with an exploration of the current state of play in Ukraine and the legacy of Soviet regulation. It also explores some of the weaknesses and inefficiencies that currently face the permitting based system. The chapter draws upon the standards and experiences of EU countries and the EU as a whole as a basis for the guidance it provides. It explores the advantages and disadvantages of GBRs, the costs of developing GBRs, the estimated number of GBRs that would need to be developed in Ukraine, and the challenge of applying GBRs to existing and new facilities.

Introduction

The objective of the guidance in this chapter is to help Ukraine reform its permitting system with regard to regulating SMEs, drawing upon good practices from the EU and other OECD countries. It aims to streamline and simplify regulatory requirements for installations with low environmental impact while emphasising the integrated approach to their environmental management.

The Guidance contains general information about simplified regulatory tools, a review of current environmental regulatory practices in Ukraine, recommendations for environmental regulatory reform with respect to SMEs in Ukraine, and two sectoral case studies that provide practical examples of designing and implementing of key instruments to promote environmental compliance and green business practices among SMEs. The target audience of this document includes key government stakeholders (first of all, the Ministry of Ecology and Natural Resources and the Ministry of Economic Development and Trade), business associations as well as non-governmental and academic institutions in Ukraine.

The Guidance is broadly based on the analysis and recommendations of the EU-funded project "Air Quality Governance in the ENPI East Countries" (EU 2014) which had a special activity on regulation of installations beyond the scope of Annex I of the EU Industrial Emissions Directive and which was completed in 2014.

Current environmental regulatory framework in Ukraine

Ukraine's system for environmental regulation of economic activities was introduced in the early 1990s with air emissions permitting, which still remains its most demanding and widespread part. One of its main shortcomings is the absence of links between permitting and measurable environmental quality goals or other reliable indicators of environmental performance.

Instead of encouraging technological innovation, this environmental regulatory regime effectively sells indulgences to pollute, as it is extremely challenging for businesses to comply with overly complex and often unrealistic requirements. Environment-related permits are mostly concerned with air emissions, wastewater discharges and solid waste disposal, although Ukraine's air legislation remains the most developed and complex one with its demand of a special permit for each and every point source of emissions. For example, direct instrumental measurements of air emissions are obligatory for all point sources (except petrol stations) while for most installations it has no sense for permitting or monitoring purposes. As a result, enterprise managers focus on keeping their papers in order instead of dealing with business development and cleaner technologies.

The regulations that were originally designed for detailed technical evaluation have been transformed, with the help of a controversial system of pollution charges on thousands of parameters, into an instrument for creating and channeling financial streams. Every new piece of legislation becomes an additional argument in negotiations and fixing the price of non-compliance.

Another commonly recognised problem is the absence of appropriate differentiation between major polluters and low-risk installations. The scope of application of the permitting requirements allows certain discretion of environmental authorities, so SMEs in one sector may be subject to thorough permitting in one region but completely ignored in another.

The institutional framework for environmental permitting in Ukraine is very complex and requires approvals from a large number of government stakeholders (Figure 10.1).

The MENR has gone through a drastic institutional reform when its 27 regional offices (which had been in place from the very first days of independent Ukraine) were abolished as of 17 May 2013. This change was justified by the simplification goals of the administrative reform and by citing the experience of EU countries where regional governments deal with environmental permits. The function of permitting authorities was transferred from the oblasts (regions) to the headquarters in Kyiv for all major polluters (roughly corresponding to the IED Annex I categories), without any additional staff allocations to the Ministry. Regional administrations found themselves responsible for the environmental regulation of SMEs, without having the appropriate technical capacity.

Figure 10.1. **Main institutional responsibilities for environment-related permitting in Ukraine**

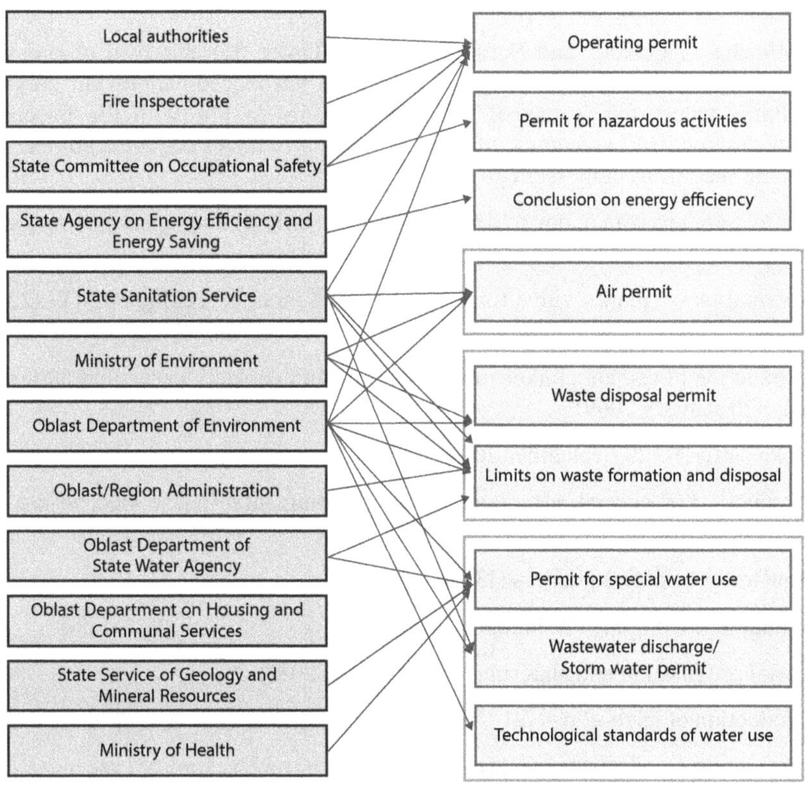

Air emissions regulation

A 2006 instruction of the Ministry of Ecology and Natural Resources divided regulated installations into three groups, the first one of which corresponds to the list in Annex I of the IPPC (IED) Directive. SMEs or installations without significant environmental impact fall into the second and third group. The second group consists of the installations that are part of the Ukrainian State Register for Air Emissions but are not included in the first group. The thresholds for the inclusion in the State Register for the listed 131 pollutants are fairly low (Ukraine Ministry of Ecology and Natural Resources 2002). For example, for particulates it is 3 t/year, and for NO_2, 1 t/year (for comparison, a similar threshold in the Czech Republic for NO_2 is much higher, 20 t/year).

The third group is only specified as "other installations", which in most cases are non-industrial facilities. However, a permit is obligatory for any of them, even though it can be obtained in a simplified procedure.

Importantly, operators cannot get the air permit without involving an authorised consulting firm whose employees have been trained at paid courses of the environment ministry. This creates a big market for consulting services and ample opportunities for corruption, which SMEs suffer from most.

Box 10.1. **Nationwide and sectoral ELVs in Ukraine**

In a permitting system inherited from the Soviet Union, any stationary source of air pollution is assessed based on dispersion modelling for comparison with sanitary standards developed for ambient air of populated areas. A few technology-based standards for boilers and gas turbines were an exception to this rule.

The Ministry of Ecology and Natural Resources Order "On approval of emission limit values for stationary sources" No. 309 of 27 June 2006 introduced nationwide, cross-sectoral emission limits values for dozens of pollutants broadly in line with the European Best Available Technique (BAT) recommendations. Its extensive tables contain a number of norms which in some sectors are impossible to comply with.

Industries were given an option to develop sector-specific technological emission standards. To date, they have been approved for 10 types of installations:

- thermal power plants with a total rated thermal input exceeding 50 MW (22 October 2008)
- production of cement clinker in rotary kilns with capacity exceeding 500 tonnes per day (20 January 2009)
- coke batteries (29 September 2009)
- production of normal corundum in ore-smelting three-phase electric arc furnaces (5 October 2009)
- sunflower husk fired boilers (13 October 2009)
- manufacture of glass (19 January 2012)
- metal ore roasting and sintering (21 December 2012)
- production of ferro-alloys (21 December 2012)
- steel production (primary and secondary smelting) with capacity exceeding 2.5 tonnes per hour (1 July 2015)
- production of lime in kilns with production capacity exceeding 50 tonnes per day (1 July 2015).

Source : Ukraine Ministry of Ecology and Natural Resources (2006), http://zakon4.rada.gov.ua/laws/show/z0912-06.

Wastewater discharges regulation

Wastewater discharges are regulated in Ukraine in line with the same principle of zero health risk norms, without taking account of their technical and economic feasibility. The methodology is aimed at ensuring water quality required for fisheries, with all water bodies of the country being designated for such water use. The permitting system for special use of water is based on provisions of the Water Code of Ukraine[1] (Law No. 213/95-BP of 6 June 1995) and Government Resolution No. 459 of 10 August 1992.[2]

Until the changes described in Section 2.3, the water permit required approvals from multiple government authorities, including the Ministry of Health, the State Water Agency, water supply and sanitation utilities ("vodokanals"), and even sometimes from large industrial installations with their own wastewater treatment plants if those also serve as communal water utilities. The approval process also involved regional departments of the State Emergency Service and the State Committee on Housing and Communal Services and, in case of groundwater sources, of the State Geology Committee. The approval procedure could vary from one region to another.

Contrary to the EU, environmental authorities in Ukraine do not regulate industrial discharges into centralised sewer systems; they issue permits only for discharges into water bodies. Moreover, Article 70 of the Water Code bans discharges on soil surface (into quarries, ravines, etc.). For factories located away from water bodies or towns, this requirement is impossible to comply with in principle, while soil contamination is not regulated by environmental authorities in Ukraine, contrary to the common regulatory practice in the EU.

Although the requirements for the quality of wastewater discharged in Ukraine are much tougher than in the EU, the actually used temporary discharge permits (issued in view of the technical infeasibility of regulatory requirements) are, on the contrary, considerably laxer than the comparable EU standards.

Recent changes in the permitting requirements

In 2011, an administrative reform was declared in Ukraine. The resulting amendments to the Law of Ukraine "On the list of documents allowing character in the sphere of economic activity" (No. 3392-VI of 19 May 2011)[3] attempted to simplify the permitting requirements, but this was not done systematically, and many references to them remained in force in different pieces of legislation.

In 2014, the State Regulatory Service of Ukraine announced the cancellation of 83 categories permitting documents[4]. In relation to environmental protection, those included, among others:

- permits for high-risk operations
- licences for the development and adoption of standards for the discharge of pollutants into water bodies
- approval of location of plants and facilities whose activities are related to the use of water resources and can adversely affect their status
- endorsement of a permit for special water use by state water agency in the case of surface water, by state geology authorities in the case of groundwater
- permits for construction or modification of waste management facilities
- permits for waste storage and disposal
- approval of limits on generation, storage and disposal of wastes
- permits for the production of electricity and heat from alternative energy sources
- approval of location of plants and facilities that adversely affect the condition and reproduction of forests.

As can be seen from this list, Soviet-style limits on the generation and disposal of waste were suspended, while numerous restrictions on the handling of hazardous waste remain in place. The water permitting procedure has been significantly simplified under the single window concept where the permitting authority communicates itself with the relevant state institutions. This radical simplification of Ukraine's permitting system clearly reduces the administrative burden on SMEs but does not negate the need for the development and application of new regulatory standards where necessary.

Concept and scope of simplified environmental regulation

General approaches to environmental regulation of industries

Each group of industries should be regulated by a system that will be effective in protecting the environment without entailing an excessive administrative burden. The following regulatory approach is consistent with best practices in EU member states and other OECD countries:

- The largest and potentially most polluting industries should be regulated under an integrated pollution prevention and control (IPPC) system through individual (bespoke) integrated permits with conditions based on BAT in line with the EU IED Directive.
- Low-risk industries should be regulated in the first phase of reform by the existing system of medium-specific permits and gradually proceed sector by sector towards regulation by permits based on general binding rules (GBRs) that allow cross-media integration.
- Facilities with negligible environmental risk would not need any permit, but their regulation should be ensured by an environmental registration system with simple notification.

The proportionate regulation would be achieved by introducing an IPPC regulatory system for large polluting enterprises on the one hand, and by simplifying and streamlining the regulatory requirements for SMEs with low or negligible environmental impact on the other hand.

Risk-based differentiation of the regulated community

In Ukraine, Resolution of the Cabinet of Ministers No. 212 of 19 March 2008[5] defined criteria for determining the degree of risk of installations as a basis the frequency of their inspection (Table 10.1).

In contrast, in the EU, the list of priority installations for IPPC regulation was formed on the basis of existing practice of member countries, e.g. the United Kingdom, where a similar system had been introduced earlier. In one way or another, the task of ranking industries depending on their environmental impact requires an expert assessment of data available. A formalised method of economic sector prioritisation has been proposed by the OECD to countries of Eastern Europe, Caucasus and Central Asia with use of a ranking system of conditional scores and weights (OECD 2005).

Table 10.1. **Differentiation of installations in Ukraine by degree of environmental risk**

Degree of risk	Criteria for determination	Frequency of planned inspections
High	Installations with high environmental hazard or potentially dangerous ones that deal with of I and II class hazardous substances, or transport of dangerous goods or utilities, in particular, water supply and wastewater treatment, and waste management	Annually
	Activities that causes air emissions more than 5 000 tonnes/year, water consumption and sewage – over 25 000 m³/year, generation and disposal of I and II class waste – more than 100 tonnes/year, or other waste – more than 1 000 m³/year; associated with deforestation, the use of aquatic resources, game management and the nature reserves	
Medium	Installations with high environmental hazard or potentially dangerous ones that deal with of III and IV class hazardous substances	Every 2 years
Minor	Activities that causes air emissions up to 5 000 tonnes/year, water consumption and wastewater – up to 25 000 m³/year, generation and disposal of 1 and II hazard class waste – up to 100 tons/year or other waste – up to 1 000 m³/year	Every 3 years

Practical examples from EU member states and useful international experience

Activities which could be subject to simplified regulation may be defined in one of the following ways:

1. compiling a list of activities with relevant capacity thresholds below which the environmental impact is considered low
2. establishing environmental criteria that define low environmental pollution and thus impact
3. combining the two approaches using partly a definition of activities and related capacity thresholds and partly environmental criteria.

The first approach is used, for example, in Sweden and the UK. In Sweden, activities that have intrinsically low environmental impact need only to notify local authorities. Examples of activities regulated by such a notification are:

- fish farming with production between 500 kg and 10 tonnes/year
- quarries with production below 25 000 tonnes/year
- slaughterhouses with capacity between 5 and 5 000 tonnes/year
- vegetable preparation with capacity between 10 and 1 000 tonnes/year
- mixing and bottling of liquor and wine
- textile dyeing with capacity of up to 200 tonnes/year
- tanneries with capacity between 1 and 100 tonnes of hides/year
- asphalt plants
- glass production with capacity of up to 100 tonnes/year
- motor sport tracks
- gasoline stations.

In the UK, there is a special list of waste treatment activities which are exempt from permitting requirements and which need to be registered with the local authority.

The Netherlands has extensive experience in the use of GBRs, applying them to all or some aspects of operation of installations. The rules contain an overall package of provisions and are issued by the national government, but inspection and enforcement is undertaken by local authorities. This type of regulatory approach has been positively received by both competent authorities and industry. It applies to several types of installations, including:

- construction companies
- dairy farms
- crop farms
- dry cleaning companies
- petrol stations.

In addition to these, the following types of installations under threshold values of Annex I of IED may be considered for simplified permitting under GBRs:

- combustion installations with rated thermal input of no more than 50 MW
- furnaces producing small quantities of pig iron, 2.5 tonnes per hour or less
- ferrous metal foundries melting 4 tonnes per day or less
- installations for bulk storage, blending and mixing of cement
- small scale electrolytic plating baths
- ceramics manufacturing installations with production capacity below 75 tonnes per day
- small-scale municipal solid waste incinerators (with capacity of 3 tonnes/hour or less)
- other industrial installations outside the integrated permitting regime.

An example of the low impact activities defined by the environmental criteria is given in the OECD Guidelines (OECD, 2005):

- *Air emissions*: Releases of any particular substance from the whole installation into the air should not be significant. For example, the U.S. Environmental Protection Agency defines "minor" sources of air pollution (which usually do not require a permit) as those that have no toxic air emissions and emit less than 100 tonnes per year of non-toxic air pollutants.
- *Wastewater discharges*: The installation should not release more than 20 m3 of treated wastewater on any one day into surface waters and no direct discharges into groundwater.
- *Waste generation*: The installation should not generate any hazardous waste or more than 1 tonne of non-hazardous solid waste per day, averaged over a year, and no more than 20 tonnes of solid waste on any one day.
- *Energy consumption*: The installation should not consume energy at a rate greater than 1 MW.
- *Noise*: The noise levels arising from processes and measured at the border of the installations should not exceed the existing noise level (both expressed as LAeq) by more than 3 dB.

- *Odour*: A low-impact installation should not have the potential to give rise to an offensive odour noticeable outside the premises where the installation is operated.

In Latvia, there are three categories of polluting activities that are regulated outside the scope of the EU IED Directive (category A): categories B (subject to simplified permits) and C (require a declaration) as well as those that do not fall under any of the three categories, yet are still being at least partly covered by the GBRs. The categories cover activity sectors (with some volume/size limitations). There are several regulations that prescribe ELVs for specific activities and a general procedure for determining ELVs for other activities.

Implications for compliance monitoring

The verification of compliance with all cross-media environmental permits requires cross-media inspections that would consider all relevant operational and management techniques of an installation. The differentiation of the regulated community based on environmental risk should be reflected in the frequency and depth of inspections of individual installations.

Inspectors would have to be well informed of the applicable GBRs and should be consulted when setting up permit conditions to make them more realistic and enforceable. In some cases it may be necessary to invite specialists from other agencies, especially if sectoral GBRs cancel specific permits that those agencies were in charge of. The inspection of installations that will be regulated by the registration system should be simplified, made less frequent and random.

Permitting through general binding rules

The objective of the GBR-based permitting is to regulate activity sectors rather than consider each installation individually. The following features are desirable in a permitting system for SMEs:

1. Operators should be encouraged to move away from end-of-pipe technologies for reducing discharges to air or water and adopt integrated operation and maintenance solutions, including effective environmental management techniques.
2. The permitting procedure should reduce the amount of information the permitting authority has to review and the degree of detailing needed in each case.
3. The permitting process should be transparent and easy for the operator and the general public to understand, by reference to published guidance or rules for particular classes of installations. Operators should be able to see that they are being treated fairly compared to others. The process of producing pertinent general rules or guidance must be open to comments by the public and other stakeholders.
4. A simplified system has to offer the same approach between sectors and should be proportionate to the level of environmental risk.
5. Permit conditions should, wherever possible, be consistent with business practices for a given category of installations. For example, monitoring and reporting requirements based on process data (energy or water consumption, materials use, etc.) should be reasonably preferred to instrumental measurements, as the latter are much more expensive.
6. Permit conditions must be clear, and the permitting authority must have powers to inspect its compliance.

The EU IED (Article 3, paragraph 8) defines GBRs as "emission limit values or other conditions that are adopted with the intention of being used directly to set permit conditions". These criteria could refer to a specific sector or have broader applicability.

Advantages and disadvantages of GBRs

Key advantages of GBRs include:

- adoption of uniform emission standards (statutory ELVs)
- a simplified application procedure and forms, resulting in reduced bureaucracy
- transparency, predictability and consistency
- uniform monitoring requirements, facilitating compliance assurance
- no potential to distort competition within an industrial sector
- reduced costs for the regulator (although the development of GBRs requires initial resource investment) and the operator
- limited opportunities for corruption through reduced discretion for the regulators.

At the same time, GBRs bring a number of disadvantages compared with site-specific permits:

- GBRs are not as flexible as site-specific permits with individual conditions (e.g. they cannot easily take into account local environmental conditions).
- Public participation takes a different form, as permit conditions are not site-specific and the consultation occurs only at the GBR design stage, where the possibility of changes forced by the public is less than for individual permits.
- The prescribed techniques are fixed until the GBR is reviewed, and permitting authorities can do little to impose further improvements.
- GBRs may not fit well with the implementation of economic instruments of environmental protection, such as emissions trading. Those instruments, to have an incentive impact, require the operator to have some flexibility in establishing operating conditions, whereas GBRs specify conditions precisely.

Types and coverage of GBRs

There are a number of practical criteria that should be met for the development of GBRs to be feasible:

- A GBR must cover a sufficient number of installations in a given sector for the resources used to develop it to be outweighed by the benefits from reduced effort on individual permit determinations. It is difficult to suggest specific thresholds for appropriate use of a GBR under this criterion, as in each particular country they will depend on the geographical distribution of such installations, their size, the capacity and costs of designing GBRs, etc.
- GBRs can cover all environmental aspects or they can be specific for individual media – e.g. air protection issues or waste issues.
- GBRs can only apply to well-defined categories of installations that use similar, widely accepted technologies that are unlikely to change rapidly. A GBR establishes

standard requirements for technologies and techniques to be followed. In cases where GBRs need to be frequently revised in order to accommodate changes in technology, there is no advantage to their use. At the same time, a GBR may be an effective method for introducing technological improvement in a sector.

- Installations within each category subject to a GBR should have a relatively uniform impact on the environment. If the installations' environmental impact is largely site-specific (i.e. depends significantly on local conditions), the imposition of standard conditions is unfeasible.
- It is important that the operators of installations targeted by a GBR be well organised so that their views are coherent and well expressed. GBRs will need to be developed in negotiation between the national environmental authority and the industrial sector's representatives. An industry (trade) association can be a good partner in this case.

GBRs can be developed as:

- generic (for example, general emission limit value for dust for various/all air emission sources) – these are is often too general and poorly adapted to individual industries
- sector-specific, which may not cover all the sectors but only those with many installations and fairly standard processes, e.g. combustion installation or farms
- activity-specific, which applies a cross-cutting approach, e.g. GBR for fuel combustion, cooling, waste management, etc.

The most widely used GBRs are the generic and sector-specific ones. They should address in a comprehensive way the sources of environmental impact and the techniques to minimise it.

Sector-specific GBRs should cover the following issues:

- currently applied processes and techniques
- current emissions and resource consumption levels
- production and management techniques to be used in installations subject to that GBR
- numerical limits for releases of particular substances (ELVs), where appropriate
- self-monitoring and reporting requirements.

The GBR may include an application form tailored to fit the particular type of installations under consideration.

The priority in developing first GBRs should be given to industry sectors with the biggest number of installations (to achieve the biggest reduction of administrative costs upfront) and with the strongest industry associations (to facilitate the GBR development process).

It is important to distinguish between GBR requirements for existing and for new installations. GBR may set out "new plant standards" and incorporate upgrade requirements for existing installations, in which case they would act as a stimulus for improved environmental performance. If the GBRs do not differentiate between requirements for new and existing installations, existing ones should be given a grace period of up to three years to comply with the GBR requirements, depending on the sector (this grace period should be specified in the GBR itself).

A key issue is whether a GBR is absolutely binding for the regulator and/or the operator. This should be clear in the statutory document that establishes the GBR. To be absolutely binding, the GBR must address the full range of technologies used within the given category of installations, and local environmental concerns should not be expected to raise a problem.

An alternative approach is to allow for an opt-out to the use of a GBR in favour of a full integrated permit. This might be initiated by the operator (e.g. when alternative techniques are preferred that are not addressed by the GBR) or by the regulator (e.g. to ensure that sensitive local environment is protected). If fully integrated permitting is undertaken, all the advantages (especially cost savings to the operator and the regulator) of a GBR would be lost. So it is not feasible to have a GBR for a category of installations, if their significant share would opt-out. However, if opt-outs are allowed, the operator must not be able to seek exemption from individual GBR requirements and would have to follow the full integrated permitting procedure (which may well result in stricter permit conditions).

Box 10.2. **Example of GBR conditions: UK guidance for small combustion units**

For small combustion units less 20 MW T.I. (in aggregate for multiple units) the following conditions should be set, unless there is a reason to set specific conditions (e.g. within an Air Quality Management Area).

1. No limit values on air emissions;
2. For natural gas firing: a minimum monitoring requirement of once per year for NOx (mg/m^3); O_2 (%); CO (mg/m^3), except that for very small units (< 3 MW T.I.) forming part of the aggregation the monitoring may be waived. Performance of such units would normally be managed through the requirement to adequately maintain plant;
3. For oil firing as a standby fuel:
   - Heavy fuel oil: a fuel sulphur limit of 3% (1% after 31 December 2002);
   - Gas oil: a fuel sulphur limit of 0.2% (0.1% after 31 December 2007);
4. For oil firing as primary fuel: as for (1), (2), (3) plus additional monitoring requirement of articulates;
5. For Coal firing as primary fuel: as for (4) plus a limit on sulphur in the coal burnt of 1% by weight as certified by the supplier;

This note does not apply to any units that are burning waste as a fuel.

Source : Environment Agency, England and Wales.

Procedure for developing GBRs

The environment ministry, in collaboration with ministries responsible for industry, agriculture, and other concerned sectors, should identify categories of industrial activities where within each installation the same activities are carried out, or where there are few alternative methods of carrying out these activities and where the best practices are clearly identified.

The development of GBRs can be undertaken by sector-specific institutions on the basis of:

- EU BREFs, in parts relevant to installations outside the scope of integrated permitting
- existing industry standards of good practice published either by government bodies or by industry associations (where such standards are seen as appropriate), both domestically and internationally
- national statutory ELVs, other norms and operational requirements.

A draft GBR should be sent for comments to the stakeholder authorities and discussed with representatives of the industry concerned, and their comments should be taken into account. In fact, it is useful to involve industry representatives in the drafting process already in the early stages.

The production of a GBR should also include public consultation. However, the nature of such consultation is different from that for an individual permit. Comments on a draft GBR (at the national level) would most likely come from environmental NGOs. The draft GBR should be posted on the environment ministry's website, and a notice to that effect published in a general distribution newspaper as well as in relevant industry journals. It is important that the process be seen as transparent by the general public. After public consultation, the GBR needs to be promulgated in a regulation (secondary legislation).

The introduction of a GBR system will also require that national authorities prepare technical rules for a number of categories of installations. For each category of industrial installations identified to be suitable for GBR regulation (the identification process itself is likely to take several months), the development of a GBR is likely to take between six months and one year. Therefore, the entire process may take between 3 years for the first categories of SMEs and 10 years for the full intended coverage of the system.

As techniques improve, the GBRs will need to be reviewed and amended using the same procedure as outlined above. A revised GBR must include an upgrade timetable for installations permitted under the old GBR. There can be no fixed review periods for GBRs, but they should not be revised more frequently than the term of permits issued under those rules (5-7 years). Amending GBRs could require considerable resources both from the national environmental authority and industry, as all respective permits would have to be reviewed as well. This is why this method of regulation is most suitable where techniques are likely to improve only slowly.

Legal framework for GBRs

As changes are made to the existing primary environmental legislation concerning the regulation of large pollution sources, it would also be appropriate to provide for simplified permitting regimes for other installations. The applicability criteria for each option (GBR-based and medium-specific permits) should be laid out either in a separate law on permitting of SMEs (which must appropriately define this term for the purposes of environmental regulation), or in a section of a law on integrated permitting (if a country chooses to adopt one), and/or in amendments to other environmental laws. The same laws should be used to set transitional periods for the introduction of GBRs, stipulate general requirements for self-monitoring and reporting, and the terms of validity and revision of the respective authorisations.

The competent authority for permitting SMEs should also be designated in the legislation. It is likely to be different for different permitting schemes. For GBR-based and media-permitting, the permitting authority should be the same competent environmental authority (regional or, in some cases, national) that is responsible for integrated permitting so as to avoid the existence of parallel permitting authorities. Since GBRs are themselves products of a multi-stakeholder process, decisions on individual GBR-based permits should be made exclusively by the permitting authority. Media-permitting should also be the prerogative of environmental authorities, as is currently the practice.

Permitting procedure

The procedure should designate internal responsibilities and step-by-step actions of permitting authority staff as well as stipulate interactions with the applicant, statutory stakeholders, and the public. A simple standard application form should also be designed.

Developers of a permitting procedure must make sure that it does not come into conflict with any primary or secondary legislation. The permitting procedure should also complement and not contradict existing procedures for environmental assessment, building permit issuance, and compliance assurance (inspection) and enforcement. The basic procedure can be based on the steps outlined below (the description provides also indicative number of days for different tasks).

Pre-application activities

It is important that not too much time be allotted to this stage. However, the operator may ask the permitting authority for a pre-application meeting to discuss any applicable rules and binding limits and issues to be addressed in the application.

Application

A permit application under a GBR (which may include a specific application form) serves to justify that the installation complies with all the requirements of the GBR. It should include the main items of an integrated permit application but to a lower degree of detail:

- identification of the installation
- identification of the operator
- description of the installation's activities
- operational and management techniques (to show that they conform to the specific GBR requirements)
- emissions (to demonstrate compliance with statutory limits stipulated in the GBR)
- environmental impacts (brief description or reference to the findings of an environmental impact assessment (EIA) if one has been performed for the installation)
- other relevant information.

There may be an administrative fee required to be paid with the application to cover the costs of processing it by the permitting authority.

Receipt and initial check of application

The Designated Administrator at the permitting authority should check that the application has addressed all the required questions and open a working file. Then the Responsible Official should look at the basic adequacy of the answers presented. For applications based on a GBR both checks should be fairly quick, as the GBR determines a limited number of issues that should be addressed. These checks are intended to ensure only that an application meets at least minimum requirements before the determination process begins. It is in no sense a determination of whether to issue a permit or what conditions ought to apply. The initial check of the application should take no longer than 5 days.

If an application is found not to be valid at this stage, it should be returned immediately. The Designated Administrator should attach a note to indicate where the application falls short of what is required.

Within 5 days of the application being deemed valid, the Responsible Official should decide if any major pieces of additional information are needed to ensure that the environmental quality standard will be complied with. The Designated Administrator would advise the applicant in writing and give him 10 days to respond. If this information is not received, the application should be refused. Requests for additional information should only be made in exceptional cases, as the application should respond to the requirements clearly stated in the GBR.

Consultation

The consultation process in permitting under a GBR regime is generally confined to issues of local environmental quality (consultation with the local authority) and prior compliance record by the applicant (consultation with the environmental inspectorate and local public health authorities). These stakeholder authorities may have information that could help the permitting authority to judge whether the application is truthful and accurate. They may also comment on the past performance of the operator or on possible challenges to the environment in the general vicinity of the installation (e.g. the presence of other significant sources of pollution). However, comments on the technique to be used will not be relevant as they have been decided in the GBR.

Within 10 days from the date the application was deemed valid, the Designated Administrator should send copies of the application to the stakeholder authorities with a cover letter specifying the inputs that would be helpful and asking to provide their responses within 15 days. There is normally no general public consultation for applications of GBR-governed installations, although eventually the permit itself should be put in the permitting authority's permit register.

The Designated Administrator should note all responses from the stakeholder authorities in the Working File and inform the Responsible Official. If a body fails to respond, the Responsible Official may use his judgment to decide either to seek such a response or proceed without it.

Assessment of application and determination of permit conditions

Determination

For a simple application that is in accordance with the GBR it is unlikely that it would need to be considered by a "permit team" at the permitting authority, as the different cross-media issues will have been addressed during the development of the GBR. However the Responsible Official may need to seek advice from other permitting authority colleagues where the application is for an installation in a sensitive location where compliance with the environmental quality standard is or maybe under threat.

For the application's assessment it is recommended to develop a checklist for compliance with GBRs and local environmental quality standards.

There is no need for the permitting authority to consider the merits of any alternative techniques, as all this work has been done in designing the GBR. This will substantially reduce the permitting authority's effort compared with integrated permitting. Usually, a GBR-based application should be assessed within 10 days of the receipt of the consultation responses.

Issuance

Once the application has been considered for compliance with the GBR and there are no serious objections by permitting and stakeholder authorities during consultation, the permit should be written and signed by the Responsible Official. The Designated Administrator would then send the permit to the operator and place a copy of it in the permit register. The effective date would usually be the same as requested in the application. The validity of the permit is recommended to be at least 5 years. The permit should be renewed under a simplified procedure if the original characteristics of the installations have not changed.

As the permit reflects the GBR, it is possible to include some of the rules as conditions or, simply refer to the GBR and thus produce a standard, highly simplified, permit for the sector. The permit should include numerical limits from the GBR (ELVs, limits on the use of water and/or other resources) and contain requirements to monitor and report the actual releases and any accidental discharges beyond these limits. Compliance with GBR-based permit conditions should be verified through regular environmental inspections which would, however, be much less frequent than those of large industrial installations.

Refusal

If the application's assessment (using the check-lists mentioned above) results show that further conditions are needed to protect local environmental quality, the Responsible Official may decide to refuse the application under the GBR and instruct the operator to submit another permit application. Such an opt-out by the permitting authority should only be possible if allowed by the applicable regulations and would require an approval by the head of the permitting authority's permitting department.

If the application fails to show compliance with the GBR, the Responsible Official should refuse the application. The criteria for refusal include the following:

- The environmental impact would be unacceptable within the conditions specified in the GBR (a full integrated permitting process may be required).
- The operator's proposals do not comply with specific GBR requirements.
- It is apparent that the operator cannot comply with the permit conditions because his inability to demonstrate the appropriate management systems or competence.

If the application is refused, the Designated Administrator should advise the applicant, noting the details and deadline for appeal, and copy this notice to the permit register and the stakeholder authorities, specifying the reasons for refusal.

Appeal

The applicable regulations may provide that any person or body, including the applicant for a permit, can make an appeal to the national environmental authority or to an arbitration court either against a refusal to grant a permit or against a decision to grant a permit (on the grounds that the operator cannot comply with local environmental quality standards). However, there can be no appeal against specific conditions that are set by reference to the statutory GBR.

The regulation may specify that an appeal must be made within 30 days of the permitting authority's decision on the permit and may require it to describe the grounds for the objection and the reasons, considerations, and arguments on which they are based and be accompanied by whatever documents the objector considers necessary. The permit should not enter into force until the appeal is settled. The operator should be advised of this without delay.

Timeline of the procedure

It is good practice to set out a period within which the permitting authority will normally determine a valid application. The permitting authority would normally determine a valid GBR-based application within days of its submission. The following Table 10.2 illustrates the timeline for the simplified permitting process under a GBR. However, an appeal of the decision may more than double the length of the process.

Table 10.2. **The timeline for the issuing of GBR based permit**

Period	Application review
5th day	Initial check of application is completed by the Designated Administrator and the Responsible Official *
15th day	Application is accepted and delivered by the Designated Administrator to stakeholder authorities
30th day	Consultation responses are received from stakeholder authorities
40th day	Assessment of the application is completed by the Responsible Official
45th day	Permit or refusal notice is issued
75th day	Possible appeal(s) is received by [national environmental authority] against the decision
105th day	Appeal(s) is determined
110th day	Final decision is issued by the permitting authority to the applicant. End.

* If significant additional information is needed, and the Responsible Official sends to the applicant a request that delays the process by up to 10 days.

The recommendations are derived from experience with implementation of GBR regulatory systems in EU. It is assumed that functions and responsibilities of the GBR permitting authority will cover only permitting under the GBR permitting regime. The enforcement of GBR permits will be carried out by specialised enforcement authority (e.g. environmental inspectorate), and GBR development will be arranged by specialised external experts or institutions.

Institutional requirements for the GBR-based permitting regime

The GBR-based permitting regime should complement both the proposed integrated permits and the existing media-based system. The aim of GBR system is to cover industrial and agricultural sectors with significant number of plants and operators in order to decrease the administrative burden both for facility operators and for the authorities. So, the GBR permitting authority can be the same as the integrated permitting authority or modified existing permitting authorities.

As for the organisation within the competent environmental authority itself, the task of handling of different permitting schemes for large and smaller installations favours the establishment of media-permitting departments within the permitting authority. This would allow environmental authorities to pool human and technical resources and better organise the processing of permit applications. For example, while there may be different responsible officials for handling integrated, GBR-based and media permits, the support staff (designated administrators) may be shared. In cases where for political reasons the existing media departments' structure are kept, one of these departments would have to be made responsible for processing GBR-based permit applications.

Work scope of GBR authority

The permitting authority will be responsible for:

- administration of the GBR permitting procedure
- conducting regular, planned permit review and variation of permit conditions
- maintain and operate a system for publication and storage of documents from permitting procedure
- co-operation with the inspection and enforcement authority (if separate)
- collect a fee for issuing a GBR permit (if any).

In cases where the permit writers have insufficient technical knowledge and experience to assess the accuracy of proposed permit conditions and compliance with the GBR, it may be useful to require technical support in the form of an application review by technical experts from the relevant environmental authority. The result of the review can be comments on proposed permit conditions which will be in the form of recommendations to the permit writer.

Organisational and staff requirements

The management and organisation of the GBR authority will depend on whether GBRs will cover more than one environmental medium and if the GBR authority will be set up along with the integrated permitting authority. This will infer from the current distribution of permitting functions and shall be specially stipulated in the environmental permitting. Generally there are the following possibilities where to place the GBR permitting function:

a. environment ministry at the central level
b. environment ministry at the regional level
c. environmental inspectorate
d. regional authorities
e. local authorities.

Placing the GBR permitting in the central office of the environment ministry is recommendable for small countries where the current permitting is ensured by the Ministry's central office and where the number of installations falling under the GBR permitting regime will be up to 500.

Placing the GBR permitting in regional offices of the environment ministry is recommended for bigger countries where the regional offices ensure currently environmental permitting and where the number of installations falling under the GBR permitting regime will be more than 200 per region.

Placing the GBR permitting in the environmental inspectorate is recommendable for countries where either the current permitting is ensured by the inspectorate or where environmental inspectors are the only technically capable resources to cope with GBR permitting.

Placing the GBR permitting in regional authorities is recommended for bigger countries where the regional authorities already have some experience with environmental permitting and where the number of installations falling under the GBR permitting regime will be more than 200 per region.

Placing the GBR permitting in local authorities is recommended for large countries where municipalities ensure currently some environmental permitting/approvals and where the number of installations falling under the GBR permitting regime will be over 400 per region.

There is no need for special organisational set up. The organisation can be the same for any decentralised level (i.e. regional offices of the environment ministry, regional or local authorities, or the inspectorate). Based on the experience in EU countries, there is a need of approximately one permitting officer per 50-80 installations. Thus the GBR authority on regional or county level shall be part of either the existing permitting departments or part of the integrated permitting department. The GBR permitting team shall include permitting officers and a co-ordinator/manager. There should be established co-operation with media departments which are responsible for air protection, water and waste permits in case of need for consultations.

Registration of installations with low environmental impact

For installations with insignificant environmental impact, registration can act as permission to perform their activities. Such registration can be seen as simple notification procedure for local municipal or environmental authorities. The choice of registration authority will depend on each country's institutional structure.

In case of registration, the information about such installations would be available to environmental authorities at a minimal administrative cost (for example, by using online registration services). By contrast, exempting small polluting installations from regulation altogether may bear a risk that environmental authorities are unaware of their existence, which would leave significant scope for uncontrolled pollution.

The legislation has to specify clear criteria for classification/determination of relevant installations. The criteria/thresholds can determine the amount and nature of emissions in general or provide specific values for different sectors or activities as well as include capacity thresholds. In case the criteria are sector-specific, it is necessary to consult the representatives of this industrial sector in order to understand the actual and potential impact from installations and activities in question.

Designation of the administrative body for issuing the registration

The administrative body responsible for the registration procedure has to be designated in the environmental permitting legislation with a list of all main powers and functions of the registration authority. The following responsibilities and tasks are proposed for the registration authority for implementation of the registration system:

- perform the registration procedure and establish relevant administrative mechanism within the authority
- ensure the use of electronic registration system in order to enable a national database of registered installations.

Detailed provisions for the registration procedure can be included in the implementing legislation.

Requirements for operators

The operator should be able to demonstrate to the regulator that, given the nature of the installation's activities, the criteria of insignificant environmental impact will be met without having to rely on a significant management effort. If the installation depends, for example, on abatement equipment (scrubbers, filters, etc.), it is unlikely that it can be treated as having only a low potential for impact as failure of these could clearly result in significant releases. It should be able to meet the criteria differentiating small polluting installations from medium polluting installations.

New small polluting installations should be required to submit an environmental registration form at the same time as they apply for an operating licence. Existing small polluting installations that are currently required to obtain environmental permits should be notified by the competent authority that they no longer need to have a permit but have to submit a registration form. Existing installations that presently do not need a permit should be also registered.

The registration should not have a validity limitation, but the operator should be required to notify the competent authority of any changes to the installation's activities or their cessation. If the installation does not meet some criteria for intrinsically low impact, the official should notify the operator about a need to apply for an environmental permit without which it cannot continue to operate the installation.

Information and methodological support for the registration system at the central level

The registration system has little requirements for methodological support and information, nevertheless some basic information and guidance is needed. The support should be provided at the central level by the environment ministry and its regional offices where relevant.

The appropriate functioning of the registration system requires the following information and tools:

- legal provisions for the registration procedure and related issues, criteria for small polluting installations, requirements for operators, duties of registration authorities and possible sanctions
- an electronic database for registration of small polluting installations
- a registration form
- a checklist for verification of the filled registration forms.

The registration form for small polluting installations has to be very simple, while making specific reference to the regulation authorising such registration. It should normally include the following:

- name and address of the operator
- location of the installation
- brief description of activities carried on it
- the nature and amount of any polluting releases from the activities (solid, liquid or gaseous) and a statement that they comply with the criteria for intrinsically low impact
- the maximum rate at which energy is used by the activities carried on
- a statement that no offensive odour from its activities is present outside the installation
- a statement that noise levels outside the installation arising from the activities do not increase background levels by more than 3 dB Leq.

Registration procedure

The registration procedure has to be outlined in the environmental permitting legislation, and details can be specified either in an implementing regulation, or some procedural steps can be applied based on the administrative code.

A registration officer of the competent environmental or municipal authority should check completeness of the application. If some information is missing, the form should be returned immediately indicating in written where additional information is required. If the form is complete, the official should decide whether it the installation meets all criteria for intrinsically low impact. In some cases the simplified public consultation can be held.

The registration procedure shall be a simple check of compliance with the inclusion criteria for registration based on the registration form with necessary annexes confirming for example the scope of air emissions or wastewater contamination. On regular basis the state of registrations shall be reported to the relevant oblast environmental offices and inspectorate.

In case of a positive conclusion, the officer should make a respective record in an appropriate database. If the registration is managed by the municipal authority, there should be a procedure to share the information from this database with the relevant environmental authority.

The removal of low polluting installations from the existing permitting and approval system will result in a certain decrease of the workload of the existing permitting authorities.

Institutional requirements for the registration regime

Registration authorities shall have the following functions and responsibilities:

- administration of the registration procedure for existing and new installations
- recording new and updated registrations in the national electronic register and reporting on the progress
- communication with environmental inspectors in case of unclear categorisation of a low-risk installation.

The environmental registration of enterprises or activities with low environmental impact does not require extensive technical expertise and thus the registration procedure can be carried out either at the local level of state administration or at the regional level. The registration could be running parallel to business registration. Generally, there are the following possibilities where to place the registration function:

a. the registration authority can be in the same authority as the existing permitting authority (e.g. within departments of the environment ministry at the central or regional level).

b. the registration function can be delegated to regional or municipal authorities which are not issuing any environmental related permits in the existing system, but which are issuing business registration.

In case the registration function is within the existing permitting authority, some of the permitting officers which have been dealing with issuing permits or approvals will be responsible for administering registration. This solution has the advantage of technical and administrative knowledge in checking the correctness of the registration form. Nevertheless, in case this authority is not at the same time responsible for the business registration, the simplification of the administrative burden for the relevant operators will be limited, since the operator of low polluting installation will have visit another authority apart from business registration.

In case the registration function is in a municipal authority, it will be more convenient for the operators, but the staff of the authority will need to be more thoroughly trained in order to assess the information in the environmental registration form. Nevertheless, this can be overcome by proving the low environmental impact by existing operators through the last environmental or operational permits and arrange possible consultations with the relevant department at the environment ministry responsible for the registration system.

It is envisaged that there will be no need for any additional staff in the municipal/local authorities to ensure the registration function in case of connecting this registration with existing business registration.

Implementation of simplified environmental regulation in Ukraine

As discussed in Section 3.1, two different regulatory regimes for low-risk installations that represent the vast majority of SMEs are proposed: introduce a notification procedure for registration of installations with negligible risk and gradually substitute medium-specific permits by sector-specific or nationwide GBRs. The details of the design of each regime are presented in Sections 4 and 5.

Although the simplification of permitting for SMEs will be less resource-intensive than the establishment of an integrated permitting system for high-risk installations in line with the EU IED, it will also require certain legal and institutional adjustments that will take time.

Scope of legal review

The MENR, in collaboration with the MEDT, the Ministry of Fuel and Energy, the Ministry of Health, the State Agency on Energy Efficiency and Energy Saving, other government agencies should identify categories of industrial activities where within each installation the same activities are carried out, where there are few alternative methods of carrying out these activities and where the best practices are clearly identified.

The MENR should consider industrial activities listed in Annex I of the IED but below the production capacity thresholds listed there, as well as other activities currently regulated by media-based environmental legislation. Such comprehensive assessment based on best practices would require a significant effort. The MENR of Ukraine would also need to undertake an analysis of the impact of introduction of GBRs from the legal, procedural, institutional and financial points of view in order to establish the necessary prerequisites for its smooth implementation. A government regulation should also establish criteria to be used to assess the level of environmental risk of any particular installation to determine its eligibility for registration. Tables 10.3 and 10.4 provide suggestions for specific categories of installations to be subject to GBR permitting and registration regimes based on a review (EU Neighbours East 2014) of practical experience of Latvia and other EU member-countries' best practices.

The proposed streamlining and simplification changes are connected with third-level legal documents of ministries and state agencies. But the legal review should be undertaken in the overall context of the ongoing harmonisation of the national legislation with that of the EU, in particular of the implementation of IPPC, preferably in the framework of a law on environmental permitting. Such "codifying" of requirements for operators in one piece of legislation would also require corresponding amendments to media legislation and other regulations stipulating permits related to environmental protection.

The legal review should also determine which permits and approvals would be cancelled with the implementation of GBRs specific sectors.

Costs and benefits of introducing a simplified regulatory system

Costs of adaptation to a simplified regulatory system

The institutional transformation towards the registration system shall impose the following costs:

a. reorganisation costs related to the preparation of the GBR permitting system at the MENR (similar costs related to the preparation of the registration system would be minimal)

b. costs of training of permitting officers in issuing GBR permits

c. costs of information campaigns (via the internet or by local authorities) to inform low-risk enterprises about the registration system.

There are no significant costs related to the adaptation to a simplified regulatory system for low-risk enterprises. There should be no significant impact on employment in the SME community.

The appraisal of the costs of the development of GBRs can be made only based on the determination of the list of sectors which would be covered by GBRs. A preliminary estimation could be made based on the costs of developing BAT guidance and experience with GBR development in several EU countries.

It is possible to estimate that the number of sectors covered by GBRs will equal at a minimum the number of EU BREFs, as they would cover the same activities as the IPPC regulation but with lower capacity thresholds, as well as other activities with significant pollution to any of the environmental media. The cost of preparing GBRs for one sector would range from EUR 10 000 to EUR 20 000 depending on the complexity of the sector concerned.

As it is proposed to assign the function of registration to local authorities in conjunction with business registration, environmental authorities would have less work, while for local authorities the new registration responsibility would not bring excessive work load or require additional financial resources.

Benefits of regulatory simplification

The introduction of a GBR permitting system will increase the transparency of the administrative permitting procedure and, as a result, will likely reduce opportunities for corruption. The simplified one-window permitting procedure would make small entrepreneurship more attractive.

SMEs will benefit from a substantial reduction of administrative burden in terms of costs of environmental consulting services and those related to obtaining or renewing the multiple permits and approvals that are currently required. Those SMEs that will only be subject to notification requirements will see even bigger economies.

Implementation scenarios

The period needed for the development of GBRs depends on the number of sectors brought under the GBR system and the availability of financial resources. The time schedule for GBR development will determine the timeline of the phase-in of GBR-based permitting in different sectors. Operators of eligible installations should be required to submit applications for GBR permits within two years after the approval of the relevant sectoral GBR. Furthermore, it would be practical to link the submission of a GBR permit application with the deadline for renewal of existing permits during the two-year transition period.

It is expected that the registration regime will not cause any significant administrative burden, especially if it is administered by local authorities in conjunction with business registration. A one-year transition period may be set, during which all existing low-risk enterprises will be obliged to fill a registration form and submit it to the relevant authority. The deadline for registration of existing enterprises should be set at one year after the approval and publication of the relevant implementing legislation.

In the context of an ongoing IPPC reform, the preparation of a GBR permitting system should ideally take place only after the start of the integrated permitting system implementation in order to have available staff and experts for the preparatory activities, such as drafting implementing regulations and developing GBRs. The preparation of the registration system should start as soon as possible.

As large industrial installations gradually convert to integrated permitting, the country's national environmental authority will have to choose appropriate permitting regimes for the installations that are not covered by the integrated permitting system. While installations with intrinsically low impact can be transferred to a registration scheme fairly quickly, the introduction of GBRs will take time and may not be appropriate for a significant number of installations. Therefore, for a number of years media-permitting will remain the default option for regulating SMEs that are either unsuitable for a GBR or scheduled to be covered by GBR at a later date.

However, once the development of all appropriate GBRs has been completed and a GBR scheme is fully operational, the MENR may consider whether it would be feasible to choose one of the three options for regulation of economic sector in question:

1. Incorporate these installations into the integrated permitting system. This may be appropriate for installations that affect more than one environmental medium but would require the development of technical guidance for them, which is a time-consuming and expensive process.
2. Develop or adjust national generic statutory ELVs that would directly apply to installations not covered by any other permitting scheme, making them a simplified version of a GBR. However, they would necessarily cover only a limited range of polluting substances and, in the absence of technique and environmental quality considerations in permitting decisions for such installations, would fall short of ensuring a high level of environmental protection.[6]
3. Keep a certain number of SMEs under a media-permitting scheme.[7] This would be feasible especially for installations that have an impact on only one environmental medium and that are technologically diverse (like medium-sized bricks production). In this case, media-permitting should be procedurally simplified, as it would at that point be used exclusively for selected categories of SMEs.

The first two options would mean a gradual phase-out of media-permitting in the country, while the third would retain it for limited use after the integrated permitting system has been fully established (which may take up to 15 years). Phasing out media-permitting may look attractive from the perspective of reducing the number of permitting schemes, but regulating the "remaining" installations under either integrated permitting or statutory ELVs will also have serious drawbacks, as mentioned above. On the other hand, keeping media-permitting as a regulatory option is likely to increase the administrative burden on the permitting authorities, as they would have to handle three different permitting processes: full integrated permitting, simplified GBR-based permitting, and media-permitting. Ultimately, a decision on the fate of the media-permitting system will be based on the medium-specific impacts and sectoral distribution of the SMEs that were deemed unsuitable for GBR.

Conclusion

Reforming Ukraine's environmental regulatory regime for SMEs is an ambitious undertaking. It will involve co-ordination and co-operation among the wide range of government actors who are currently responsible for different environment-related permitting procedures. It will also require the development of general binding rules that can remain stable for extended periods of time without being updated, and can be applicable across industries. To succeed, it will necessitate an extensive communications campaign and the establishment of effective information tools. SMEs are by definition an incredibly heterogeneous as a group, and sectoral strategies will have to be deployed to ensure that the new approach to regulating low risk facilities is understood. In some cases, SMEs that have never applied for a permit before will now have to self-report their activity.

However, the benefits are commensurate to the effort. Although Ukraine has strict environmental regulations on paper, they are not effective and difficult to enforce, and the system has resulted in confusion amongst enterprises and significant potential for corruption. Moving from a permitting system to a rules based system for SMEs could go a long way in reducing regulatory burden on SMEs, reducing the burden on the regulators themselves, and enhancing environmental performance.

Table 10.3. **Activities and installations requiring GBR-based permits**

Sector and type of activity
1. Energy industry:
1.1. Combustion installations with rated thermal input:
1.1.1. from 5 to 50 MW, if biomass (also wood and peat) or gaseous fuels are used in the combustion installation
1.1.2. from 0.5 to 50 MW, if liquid fuels are used in the combustion installation, except fuel oil (heavy fuel oil)
1.1.3. from 5 to 50 MW, if liquid fuel or fuel oil, is utilised in the combustion installation that is used in a grain dryer
1.1.4. from 0.2 to 50 MW, if coal is utilised in the combustion installation
1.2. Combustion installations in which fuel oil (heavy fuel oil) is utilised
1.3. Oil depots and terminals with 5 000 or more tonnes of fuel per year (the largest total amount of fuel pumped per year during the last three years)
1.4. Petrol stations with 2 000 or more m³ of fuel per year (the total largest amount of fuel pumped during the last three years)
1.5. Gas storage installations with a capacity of 100 m³ or more and underground storage sites of natural gas
1.6. Coal and brown-coal briquetting equipment
1.7. Production of charcoal
2. Production and processing of metals:
2.1. Installations for the production of pig iron or steel, also for continuous casting, with a capacity not exceeding 2.5 tonnes per hour
2.2. Installations for the processing of ferrous metals;
2.2.1. hot-rolling mills which process less than 20 tonnes of crude steel per hour
2.2.2. installations for the application of protective fused metal coats, which treat less than 2 tonnes of crude steel per hour
2.3. Ferrous metal foundries with a production capacity of up to 20 tonnes per day
2.4. Installations for smelting, also fusion, of non-ferrous metals, including metals to be used for recycling, the melting capacity of which does not exceed four tonnes of molten lead or cadmium per day or 20 tonnes of other metals per day, except installations that are used in crafts and sculpture, including for the processing of gold and silver
2.5. Installations in which electrolysis or chemical processes are used for surface treatment of metals and plastic materials and the total volume of the treatment vats of which does not exceed 30 m³
2.6. Installations for surface treatment during the operation of which dust is created, including the polishing of iron, steel or other metallic objects, cleaning by sand blasting and powder painting, if the total discharge of the installation is 10 000 m³ per hour or more
2.7. Floating docks and dry docks of a steel shipyard
2.8. Other installations for industrial processing of iron, steel or other metals with a production area of 1 000 m² or more
2.9. Installations for the production of cables
2.10. Installations for the production of accumulators and batteries
2.11. Electro-technical equipment for the production of transformer and printed circuits
3. Production of mineral products:
3.1. Installations for the production of cement clinker in rotary kilns the production capacity of which does not exceed 500 tonnes per day or installations for the production of lime in rotary kilns with a production capacity that does not exceed 50 tonnes per day, or in other furnaces with a production capacity that does not exceed 50 tonnes per day
3.2. Installations for the manufacture of glass, including glass fibre, with a melting capacity that does not exceed 20 tonnes per day, except craftsmanship
3.3. Installations for melting mineral substances, including the production of mineral wool, with a melting capacity that does not exceed 20 tonnes per day
3.4. Installations for the manufacture of ceramic products by firing, including roofing tiles, bricks, refractory bricks, tiles, stove tiles, pottery, faience or porcelain, in which up to 75 tonnes of finished products may be manufactured per day, except for craftsmanship
3.5. Cement production units with a production capacity of 20 000 or more tonnes per year and installations for the production of concrete and concrete products with a capacity of 20 000 m³ per year or more
3.6. Installations for the production of plaster products, except craftsmanship

Sector and type of activity
4. Chemical industry and activities with chemical substances and chemical products:
4.1. Installations for the production of organic and inorganic substances, products or intermediary products, including enzymes, in which physical production processes (for example, dilution and mixing) are utilised
4.2. Installations for the storage of unpacked organic or inorganic chemical substances, chemical products or intermediary products, if 1 tonne or more is stored, for the storage of enzymes – 20 tonnes or more
4.3. Installations for the production of pharmaceutical products, in which physical processes (for example, dilution and mixing) are utilised
4.4. Installations for the production of explosives, in which physical production processes (for example, mixing) are utilised
4.5. Installations for the production of munitions
4.6. Installations for industrial production of colorants, additives and ancillary substances (also usable in food industry), in which physical processes are utilised (for example, dilution and mixing), except retail trade
4.7. Installations for the production of chemical substances and chemical products and also for the production of plant protection products and biocides using physical methods (for example, dilution and mixing), packing and filling
4.8. Installations for the production of soaps, detergents and cleaning agents with a production capacity of 1 tonne per year or more
4.9. Installations for the production of paints, varnishes or glue
4.10. Installations for the production of goods with teflon thermo-coating, thermoplastic materials moulded by extrusion or by performing recycling of fibrous thermoplastic composite materials, if 100 kg of plastic or more are used per day
4.11. Installations for the production of plastic goods, using injection moulding from alloy, the extrusion process, including calendering or thermal moulding, if 5 or more tonnes of plastic are used per day. Installations for the production of plastic goods from expanded polystyrene, if 5 or more tonnes of plastic are used per day
4.12. Installations for the production of goods of rubber with a production capacity above 500 tonnes per year
4.13. Installations for the production of regenerated pulp
4.14. Installations for the production of gelatine and glue from the skin and bones of animals
4.15. Installations for the production of organic chemical products via chemical, biological or physical process (that are not subject to regulation in accordance with Annex I of Directive 2010/75/EU)
4.16. Installations for the production of asphalt and road surfacing materials
4.17. Installations for the production of roof covering, using tar and bitumen
4.18. Installations for the distillation of tar
4.19. Gas and coke plants
4.20. Weaveries, spinneries and knitwear production units, if the production capacity is 100 kg per day or more
4.21. Dry-cleaners
4.22. Laundries with a capacity exceeding 1 000 kg per day
5. Waste management:
5.1. Installations for the disposal or processing of hazardous waste, including petroleum product waste, the capacity of which does not exceed 10 tonnes per day
5.2. Installations for the incineration or co-incineration of municipal waste and other waste that may not be classified as hazardous waste, if the capacity of the installation does not exceed three tonnes per hour
5.3. Installations for the incineration or co-incineration of hazardous waste, the capacity of which does not exceed 10 tonnes per day
5.4. Installations for biological or physico-chemical treatment of municipal waste, the capacity of which does not exceed 50 tonnes per day, except composting installations with an intake capacity not exceeding 100 tonnes per year and composting installations for animal manure
5.5. Installations for the treatment of municipal waste for purposes of disposal in which the biological or physico-chemical treatment method is not utilised
5.6. Landfills for the processing of municipal waste with capacity not exceeding 75 tonnes per day
5.7. Landfills that can receive up to 10 tonnes of waste per day or with a total capacity not exceeding 25 000 tonnes, excluding landfills of inert waste
5.8. Landfills of inert waste
5.9. Places for the disposal, storage or composting of wastewater sludge and waste that may not be classified as hazardous waste in accordance with legislation

Sector and type of activity
5.10. Installations for the processing of discarded vehicles with capacity not exceeding 75 tonnes per day and for the recycling and storage of ship wrecks
5.11. Installations for the sorting or temporary storage of municipal waste, including reloading stations with a receiving capacity of 30 tonnes of waste per day or more
5.12. Installations for the storage of, recycling or treatment of waste of animal origin, also installations for composting and biogas installations with a receiving capacity of waste of animal or vegetable origin, including animal droppings and waste from slaughterhouses, of 30 or more tonnes per day
5.13. Installations for the storage of hazardous waste (including at the places of creation) for more than one year
5.14. installations for temporary (not more than one year) storage of hazardous waste with a total capacity not exceeding 50 tonnes, for example, reloading stations and container warehouses, excluding storage of waste for such a short period of time or in such an insignificant amount that the waste does not cause a risk to human health or the environment
5.15. Installations for the recycling of electric and electronic waste with capacity not exceeding 75 tonnes per day
6. Agriculture, forestry and wood processing:
6.1. Slaughterhouses with a carcass production capacity from 5 to 50 tonnes per day
6.2. Installations for the disposal or recycling of animal carcasses and waste of animal origin, the capacity of which is from 1 to 10 tonnes per day
6.3. Slaughterhouses with a production capacity of products of poultry origin of 5 000 or more tonnes per year
6.4. Production of matches
6.5. Production of oriented plywood panels, plywood panels or fibre plywood panels (separate types of panels or different types of panels together) with a production capacity not exceeding 600 m^3 per day
6.6. Production of furniture, if the production area is 1 000 m^2 or more
7. Food industry:
7.1. Installations for the collection, pre-treatment and processing of milk, in which the quantity of milk received is from 10 to 200 tonnes per day (average value on an annual basis)
7.2. Installations for the production of food products, in which products of animal origin (other than milk) are treated and processed and which produce from 1 to 75 tonnes of finished product per day, or which treat and process vegetable products and produce from 10 to 300 tonnes of finished product per day (average value on a quarterly basis), including:
7.2.1. the production of oils and fats of vegetable and animal origin
7.2.2. the production of beer and malt
7.2.3. the production and bottling of non-alcoholic beverages
7.2.4. installations for industrial production of starch and potato starch
7.2.5. fish meal and fish oil production units
7.2.6. sugar production units
7.2.7. the production of coffee, tea and food additives
7.2.8. grain processing
7.2.9. the production of yeast
7.2.10. the production and bottling of alcohol and alcoholic beverages
7.2.11. the conservation, filling and packaging of products of animal and vegetable origin
7.2.12. other food product production installations in which vegetables are treated and processed
7.2.13. installations for the production of fish and crustacean products, including for the production of canned, smoked and frozen products
7.3. Facilities for the production of meat meal, including bone meal, blood meal, blood plasma and feather meal production units
7.4. Production of protein and pectin
7.5. Installations for the production of tobacco products

Sector and type of activity
8. Other sectors:
8.1. in manufacturing:
8.1.1. installations for the production of paper and cardboard with a production capacity not exceeding 20 tonnes per day
8.1.2. installations for the pre-treatment of fibres and fabric (washing, bleaching, mercerisation) or dyeing, the treatment capacity of which is from 0.5 to 10 tonnes per day
8.1.3. installations for the tanning of hides and skins, in which less than 12 tonnes of finished products are produced per day
8.1.4. volatile organic compounds emitting installations, where the use of organic solvents in the installation emitting volatile organic compounds exceeds prescribed thresholds
8.2. Crematoria
8.3. Airports and airfields
8.4. Railway depot and stations that perform the functions of a freight station, marshalling station or district station
8.5. Berths of ports for the loading and unloading of cargoes into ships with gross tonnage not less than 450 tonnes
8.6. Hospitals with the number of beds above 100
8.7. Washing installations intended for the cleaning of storage and transportation receptacles and containers of chemical substances
8.8. Wastewater treatment plants with capacity of 20 m³ per day or more that drain the treated wastewater in the environment

Table 10.4. **Activities and installations to be subject to a registration procedure**

Sector and type of activity
1. Power industry:
1.1. Combustion installations with rated thermal input of more than 0.2 MW (if a permit is not required for the combustion installation in accordance with regulations on Annex I activities or non-Annex I activities requiring permit-based regulation)
1.2. Wind power stations or power station parks with the total capacity of more than 125 kW
1.3. Petrol stations with fuel amount of up to 2000 m³ per year (the total largest amount of fuel pumped during the last three years)
1.4. Gas filling stations
1.5. Oil depots with fuel amount of less than 5000 tonnes per year
1.6. Installations for the production of heating fuel from the remains of timber
1.7. Installations for the production of heating fuel from peat
2. Production and processing of metals:
2.1. Installations for surface treatment that create dust during operation, including the polishing of iron, steel or other metallic objects, sand blasting (cleaning by sand blasting) and powder painting, if the total emission of the installation is from 300 to 10 000 m³/hour
2.2. Other installations for the processing of iron, steel or other metals with a production area from 100 m² to 1 000 m²
2.3. Foundries usable in craftsmanship, also for the casting of gold and silver
2.4. Production facilities for electro-technical products, except installations for the production of transformers or printed circuits
2.5. Bonding of plastic products
3. Manufacturing of mineral products (processing of mineral substances):
3.1. Cement production units with a production capacity from 2 to 20 000 tonnes per year and installations for the production of concrete and concrete products with a capacity from 2 to 20 000 m³ per year
3.2. Installations for the production and mixing of gravel or lime mortar and installations for the crushing of stones, which are not installed at the places where the stones are obtained
3.3. Stationary installations for the production of aerated concrete, coal dust or lime-and-sand bricks

Sector and type of activity
4. Agriculture, forestry and wood processing:
4.1. Animal housings in which 10 or more animal units are bred for commercial purposes (including the storage, collection and drainage of solid manure, liquid manure, slurry and silage juice); animal housings are located in a highly sensitive territory and in which five or more animal units are bred for commercial purposes (if the animal housing does not require permit in accordance with regulations on Annex I activities)
4.2. Sawmills and wood-processing installations in which timber-cutting machinery is utilised and which process 2 000 m^3 or more round wood and timber per year; installations in which industrial chemical treatment of timber is performed, also pressure impregnation (high-pressure impregnation), vacuum impregnation (low-pressure impregnation) and protection of timber against blue stain and mould
4.3. Fish farms
5. Food industry:
5.1. Installations for the collection, pre-treatment and processing of milk, in which the quantity of milk received is from one to ten tonnes per day (average value on an annual basis)
5.2. Installations for the production of food, in which products of animal origin (excluding milk) are processed and which produce from 0.1 to 1 tonne of finished products per day, and in which products of vegetable origin are processed and from 0.5 to 10 tonnes of finished products are produced per day (average value on a quarterly basis)
5.3. Installations for the production of fish and crustacean products, including for the production of canned, smoked and frozen products, in which less than one tonne of finished products is produced per day
5.4. Smoke-houses, meat and gastronomy production units (also in shops) in which 500 kg of food products or more are produced per day
5.5. Installations for the baking of bread and industrial production of confectionery products with production capacity that exceeds 2 tonnes per day
5.6. Slaughterhouses with a production capacity of carcasses less than 5 tonnes per day
6. Other sectors:
6.1. Repair and maintenance shops for mechanical land vehicles, mobile agricultural machinery and mobile non-road machinery, and other movable aggregates, where the following activities are performed: diagnostics, maintenance and repair of motor maintenance and repair of power system installation, diagnostics and repair of electric devices and alarm systems diagnostics, maintenance and repair of transmission and elements diagnostics, maintenance and repair of suspension and steering equipment diagnostics, maintenance and repair of brake system assembly, adjustment and repair of tires and wheels body diagnostics, geometry reconstruction and repair anti-corrosion treatment of body preparation for painting and painting car wash and body maintenance.
6.2. Chemical and biological laboratories (except study laboratories)
6.3. Wastewater treatment plants with a capacity from 5 to 20 m^3 per day, if wastewater is drained in the environment
6.4. Installations and photographic laboratories in which 1 000 m^2 or more of photographic films are processed per year
6.5. Installations for the storage of salt and salt mixtures, if 1 tonne or more of salt or salt mixtures is stored, installations for obtaining salt and salt mixtures (with a capacity of 1 tonne or more per day) for scattering on roads during winter conditions
6.6. Installations for the production of casement windows and doors
6.7. Installations for the storage of packed organic and inorganic chemical substances, chemical products or intermediary products, if more than 10 tonnes of chemical substances, chemical products or intermediary products are stored

Notes

1. http://zakon4.rada.gov.ua/laws/show/213/95-%D0%B2%D1%80.
2. http://zakon4.rada.gov.ua/laws/show/459-92-%D0%BF.
3. http://zakon4.rada.gov.ua/laws/show/3392-17.
4. Official note of the State Regulatory Service of Ukraine of 10 April 2014, www.dkrp.gov.ua/info/3339.
5. Official note of the State Regulatory Service of Ukraine of 10 April 2014, www.dkrp.gov.ua/info/3339.
6. For example, a regulation of small polluting sources in the Czech Republic sets national ELVs for 10 pollutants.
7. In many EU countries that had media-permitting before the implementation of the IPPC Directive in 2007 as well as in part of the new Member States, this system has remained in place for installations that are not subject to integrated permitting.

References

EU (2014), *Recommendations for ELVs and other conditions setting for selected installations*, EuropeAid/129522/C/SER/Multi project Air Quality Governance in the ENPI East Countries (2014).

EU Neighbours East (2014), *Air Quality Governance in the ENPI East Countries project*, EU Neighbours East, http://airgovernance.eu/.

OECD (2005), *Integrated environmental permitting guidelines for EECCA countries*, Organisation for Economic Co-operation and Development, Paris (Subsection 6.4.2.1, Sector Prioritisation).

Ukraine Ministry of Ecology and Natural Resources (2006), Order No. 309, "On approval of emission limit values for stationary sources", 27 June 2006, http://zakon4.rada.gov.ua/laws/show/z0912-06.

Ukraine Ministry of Ecology and Natural Resources (2002), Order No. 177, "On approval of Instruction on procedure and criteria for the state registration of installations which have or could have harmful impact on public health and air quality", 10 May 2002, http://zakon4.rada.gov.ua/laws/show/z0445-02.

Chapter 11

Green certification scheme for SMEs in the hospitality sector in Georgia

This chapter provides a justification and detailed implementation plan for a green certification scheme for SMEs in the hospitality sector in Georgia. The chapter begins with an explanation of benefits of green certification schemes generally, before discussing Georgia's specific situation. The design and scope of a hospitality green certification scheme is explored. Guidance on institutions that should be involved in the design phase and the implementation phase is provided. Comparisons are made with certification schemes in other national jurisdictions, and different sub-sectors within the hospitality sector in Georgia are examined. Finally, criteria are proposed for the three levels of the green certifications scheme.

Introduction

A green certification scheme can harness the business opportunities provided by an environmental business model. In addition to saving money on energy and resource use, enterprises that are part of a green certification scheme will improve their image and attract more customers and, therefore, enhance their market position. Participants of green certification schemes also benefit from extra publicity, as their promotional materials and detailed information are made available on the website of the accrediting organisation. Sector specific green certification schemes can be particularly valuable, as they can have much more targeted criteria than generic cross-industry certification schemes.

Certification is defined as "a voluntary procedure that assesses audits and gives written assurance that a facility, product, process or service meets specific standards; it awards a marketable logo to those that meet or exceed baseline standards" (Honey and Rome, 2001; Georgian National Tourism Administration, 2014). Green certification schemes are applied to an entire business model and, unlike eco-labels that target green products, promote green business practices of an enterprise.

In Georgia, SMEs make up to 94.1% of all enterprises, with the hospitality sector accounting for 4.8% of all SMEs (OECD, 2014; OECD, 2015). Four main sub-sectors are distinguished based on the differences of their business models and the average size of SMEs:

- hotels and large accommodations (hotel-type accommodations that provide more than 25 rooms)
- hostels and guest houses
- restaurants, cafes and bars
- eco-tourism providers.

Developing the hospitality sector is one of the current priorities of the Georgian government. Its importance is growing with the expansion of tourism in Georgia. Over the last decade, the country's infrastructure has been improved, facilitating access to remote rural tourist destinations, creating new opportunities for local hospitality businesses. The number of foreign visitors to the country reached 5.5 million people in 2014, growing by 2% from the previous year, after a steep increase by 57% in 2012 (Georgia National Tourism Administration 2014). Raising the environmental profile of the sector and promoting eco-tourism is likely to attract even more foreign tourists and contribute to the growth of domestic tourism. One of the key instruments for doing so is green certification.

Green certification schemes are relatively easy to apply to the hospitality sector due to comparability of activities of enterprises in the sector. Green certification schemes should be designed carefully so that *the enterprise's costs of certification, including audit and certification fees as well as the cost of compliance with the certification criteria, do not exceed the commercial benefits of obtaining a green certificate*. This is particularly important in view of SMEs' lack of knowledge and human resources required to undertake environmental improvements. However, the introduction of a green certification scheme can be challenging. One major constraint is the limited capacity of SMEs (time, human resources) to fully implement the scheme.

This guidance focuses on the design and coverage of a green certification scheme, as well as award criteria and institutional arrangements for its implementation.

Design and coverage of green certification schemes

The design and coverage of a green certification scheme should take into account the nature of tourism sub-sectors: hotels, smaller guest houses, restaurants, cafes and bars or eco-tourism providers, drawing on best international practices. A multi-level structure of the scheme would facilitate the gradual adoption of these practices by SMEs in the hospitality sector.

The hospitality sub-sectors in Georgia have different business models, depending on the main activity of the enterprise. These activities can range from providing accommodation, to catering, to organising outdoor activities. Different activities have their own environmental considerations and best practices. Internationally, green certification schemes either concentrate only on one type of tourism activities (e.g. the Green Star Hotel label in Egypt is designed specifically for the hotel industry in Egypt), or cover a wide variety of tourism sub-sectors (e.g. Green Globe certifies the travel industry sector from cruise ships and golf courses to tour operators, accommodation and management companies). This guidance recommends a consolidated green certification scheme with one logo applied to all the sub-sectors. In designing this scheme, common baseline standards and requirements should be combined with the sector-specific ones.

To simplify SMEs' entry to the green certification scheme, this guidance suggests three levels of certification for hospitality sub-sectors. Each level should be measured by a performance-based set of criteria. The first level should include only basic environmental criteria, whereas to obtain the highest level an enterprise would need to implement further steps in greening its business model. Three types of criteria should be distinguished: mandatory criteria for the entire hospitality sector, divided into three progressive levels; core sub-sector criteria that reflect the specifics of businesses within the hospitality sector, also divided into three progressive levels; and optional criteria that will allow enterprises to tailor the certification scheme to their business operations, provided as a common list.

Depending on the preferences of businesses, the accreditation body (the Green Tourism Association in partnership with the National Tourism Administration), key governmental institutions (the Ministry of Economy and Sustainable Development and the Ministry of Environment and Natural Resources Protection) and consumer organisations, the levels could be designated as silver, gold and platinum, one to three green stars, or any other distinct marker or symbol.

Institutional arrangements

This section addresses institutional arrangements of two phases: *design* of the green certification scheme and its *implementation*.

Institutions and stakeholders

The accreditation body needs to be established through a public-private partnership between the competent government authorities and a major SME association in the hospitality sector in Georgia. Choosing such institutional set-up at the very beginning of the scheme's design is fundamental to its success. This will raise the credibility of the scheme and its criteria, address industry's scepticism, avoid inefficient bureaucratic processes and help attract private sector funding. The accreditation body will regulate procedures for awarding green certifications and interacting with participating enterprises throughout the implementation process. The Georgian Tourism Association (GTA) is the biggest association within the hospitality sector in Georgia, with a focus on improving the business environment in the domestic tourism sector, as well as capacity building. It has already committed itself to increasing public-private partnerships in the hospitality sector, contributing to nature protection and to projects on strengthening sustainable tourism development in Georgia, and, therefore, would be the most suitable candidate to carry out the functions of an accreditation body for the certification scheme.

The green certification scheme should receive support from the National Tourism Administration (NTA). The NTA, subordinated to the Ministry of Economy and Sustainable Development, monitors the trends in the hospitality sector's growth and development and "ensures sustainable tourism development". The data obtained from the NTA's annual and quarterly studies of the hospitality industry market can serve as a solid background for the design phase of the scheme's development. The collaboration between the GTA and the NTA could support the success of the certification scheme and be attractive to local tourism businesses. The involvement of the Ministry of Economy and Sustainable Development, the Ministry of Environmental and Natural Resources Protection as well as the Agency for Protected Areas would ensure the credibility of, and financial support for, the scheme. Consultations with local NGOs and consumers should also be institutionalised.

Design phase

The GTA would need to establish an accreditation board for the green certification scheme. The accreditation board would include representatives of the NTA, the Ministry of Economy and Sustainable Development (Department of Sustainable Development), the Ministry of Environmental and Natural Resources Protection (Department of Integrated Environmental Management), the Agency for Protected Areas, local hospitality SME Associations and NGOs, as well as any other relevant stakeholders. The accreditation board would oversee the scheme's development and implementation and verify the transparency of the scheme's procedures and financial management.

The accreditation board should order a baseline assessment of the relevant environmental legislation and a market assessment of the hospitality sector. It should also consider and approve the procedure and criteria for awarding environmental certifications, as well as an audit protocol with quantitative and qualitative checklists. Finally, it should endorse a medium-term (e.g. 5-year) financial plan, which will need to cover the green certification scheme's start-up and operating costs: design (criteria, logo, etc.), website development and maintenance, promotional materials and campaigns, training of auditors, participating enterprises, etc. Funds to support the scheme could come from a combination of public (NTA funding) or private (the GTA's network of private partner companies) sources, as well as from participation fees. Internationally, most successful schemes are financed by government and multiple private partners. Active GTA members could also benefit from discounted fees for the certification scheme (in addition to the regular annual association membership fees). It is also advised to differentiate the participation fees based on the size (annual revenue) of participating enterprises. The financial plan should envisage initial public-private funding in the design phase, with increasing revenues from participation fees in the implementation phase.

A green certification scheme's website could be based on a new or the existing GTA web platform. The website should contain detailed and easily accessible information on the scheme, the application process, fees, criteria, and participating enterprises.

Implementation phase

Once the criteria and procedures for green certification are in place, the accreditation organisation would conduct audits and issue green certificates on a continuous basis. Trainings for participating SMEs, covering the certification procedure and criteria, should be available locally and scheduled at least three times a year. Additional workshops on best practices and possible improvements of the scheme could also be conducted annually. Those enterprises that have already been trained and implemented will be able to share their experience during such events and provide feedback on the green certification scheme's design, coverage and criteria. The green certification scheme should be actively promoted through various channels: websites of the NTA, Enterprise Georgia, the Green Growth Initiative, printed promotional materials, local and international workshops and seminars, as well as through the GTA network.

Box 11.1. **Green certification schemes around the globe**

Green Hospitality Award (Ireland) – The Green Hospitality Award (GHA) is an umbrella brand that includes voluntary environmental certification schemes and eco-labels for various hospitality industry sub-sectors.

Institutional set-up: Certifying organisation – Environmental Protection Agency (EPA); partner organisations – National Tourism Development Authority (Failte Ireland), Tourism Ireland, Sustainable Authority of Ireland, Enterprise Ireland, Irish Hotels Federation, Irish Hospitality Institute, and Restaurant Association of Ireland.

Application process: Enterprises conduct a self-assessment and prepare all verification documentation. Upon payment of fees, the GHA conducts an audit and issues a certificate. Audits are conducted every 3 years to ensure compliance with GHA criteria.

Certified businesses: Hotels and large accommodation providers (including resorts and clubs), B&B's, guesthouses, self-catering and other accommodation, restaurants and bars, eco-tourism providers, attractions and activities, leisure centres and spas, SMEs – suppliers to the hospitality sector.

Levels of certification: Award (a good standard), Gold (best practice), Platinum (world class best practice, available for hotels only). Criteria becomes stricter with each level.

Fees/funding: The EPA provides funding through its Green Business Initiative. This funding is designed to help promote the award across the hospitality sector. For example, annual fees for small enterprises (revenues under EUR 75 000 per annum) are EUR 395 for the first year and EUR 295 thereafter.

Green Key (international, headquarters in Denmark) – The Green Key programme was founded in Denmark and later became a programme of the Foundation for Environmental Education (FEE). It targets strengthening of the tourism and leisure industry, environmental protection, green marketing and education of staff.

Institutional set-up: Certificates are issued by the Green Key National or International Jury. The National Jury includes representatives of the environment, health and tourism ministries, the tourism association, the association of local authorities, association of hotels and campsites, education and environmental experts.

Application process: An enterprise sends in application documents, receives and audit, on the basis of which the decision on issuing the certificate is made by Green Key National or International Jury.

Box 11.1. **Green certification schemes around the globe** *(continued)*

Certified businesses: hotels, hostels, campsites, small accommodations (B&Bs, eco-lodges, eco-farms, etc.), attractions, restaurants.

Levels of certification: no levels applicable, a point system corresponding to the percentage of criteria attained.

Fees/funding: funded by corporate partners, fees differentiate depending on the country/ region.

Green Globe Certification (international, headquarters in Australia) – Green Globe, operated in over 40 countries around the world, includes a structured assessment of the sustainability performance of travel and tourism businesses and their supply chain partners.

Institutional set-up: Differs by country and region, audits are conducted by third-party certified auditors.

Application process: Application form is submitted via the website, fees are paid to finish the registration (one year membership), advice on green practices is given to the applicant, a certificate is awarded following an audit.

Certified businesses: Attractions, meeting venues, cruise ships (river and ocean), golf courses, hotels, resorts, restaurants, spa and health centres, transportation services and car rentals, tour operators).

Levels of certification: Member (all requisite criteria), Gold Member (members certified for 5 consecutive years), and Platinum Member (members certified for 10 consecutive years).

Fees/funding: Funded through participation fees, depending on the origin and size of the company (from USD 750 for companies with under 10 employees to USD 5 000 for companies with over 250 employees).

Source : Green Hospitality Ireland (2015), www.ghaward.ie; Green Key (2015), www.greenkey.global; Green Globe (2015), greenglobe.com.

Certification procedure

An enterprise wishing to obtain a green certificate would need to choose the level most appropriate for its current business operations. As a preparatory step, the enterprise should be encouraged to conduct a self-assessment. Self-assessment instructions should be available on the green certification scheme's website. Applicants would be required to send a filled application form (available online) to the accreditation board.

The application form should be evaluated by the accreditation board upon payment of annual participation fees. The applicant should be informed about available trainings (including dates and locations). An auditor appointed by the accreditation board should be sent to evaluate the performance of the applying enterprise and check whether all criteria for the specified level have been attained. A certificate should be awarded within one month of the audit. The audit report should be available through the green certification scheme's website.

During the first three years following the certification, participating enterprises should be audited annually. Thereafter, audits should be conducted every three to five years. A participating enterprise should, however, produce and send to the accreditation board an annual report on the fulfilment of the certification criteria.

Certification criteria

Certification requirements are established through performance-based award criteria. In order to avoid "greenwashing", the requirements should be transparent (available to the public), strict but realistic, and approved by national competent authorities (the Ministry of Environment and Natural Resources Protection and/or the standardisation agency). They should also be consistent with the national legislation. It is recommended to review the criteria annually during the first three years of the scheme's implementation and every five years thereafter.

In general, enterprises should be asked to demonstrate *effective environmental management* by implementing an environmental management system tailored to the capacity of an SME (Box 11.2); and *maximisation of benefits for the environment* and *minimisation of negative impacts* by introducing resource and energy efficiency measures and other practices that help preserve the environment in local areas while reducing pollution, waste generation, noise, damage to ecosystems, etc.

Box 11.2. A simplified environmental management system (EMS)

A simplified EMS offers a feasible solution for SMEs that are willing to improve their environmental performance. This approach can be adjusted to specific needs of an SME while taking into account other factors the enterprise needs to cope with in its day-to-day activities. Generally, a simplified EMS comprises several steps/levels that allow an enterprise to get recognition for attaining the corresponding requirements. Core elements of the simplified EMS:

Level 1: Framework for environmental action – demonstrate management commitment; conduct baseline assessment; draft environmental policy; identify applicable environmental legal requirements; identify other environmental norms (codes of practice, industry standards, contractual requirements); structure all requirements by type of activity; analyse actual level of compliance; design operational control procedures to address non-compliance.

Level 2: Coherent environmental programme – evaluate aspects and impacts; make environmental policy more specific; develop objectives and targets for environmental performance; develop environmental performance indicators; define specific environmental management programmes (designate responsibilities, timeframes and resources); establish a training programme.

Level 3: Full EMS implementation – finalise internal environmental management structure; establish clear internal and external communication practices; put in place documentation and record-keeping arrangements; establish internal audit procedures; review and communicate audit findings; ensure continuous improvement of environmental performance.

Source: OECD (2015), *Promoting better environmental performance of small and medium-sized enterprises in Armenia.*

The criteria should reflect both the differentiation between hospitality sub-sectors and the multi-level approach to certification. The suggested criteria are divided into three categories: mandatory, sub-sector core and sub-sector optional. Figure 11.1 illustrates the types of criteria by level. For example, a guest house wishing to obtain a Level 1 certificate would need to comply with mandatory criteria for Level 1 and "Hostels and guest houses" sub-sector criteria for Level 1 and choose several criteria form the list of optional criteria. If this guest house decided to further apply for Level 2 certification, it would need to satisfy all the criteria for Level 1 and comply with mandatory criteria for Level 2 and "Hostels and guest houses" sub-sector criteria for Level 2 and choose several criteria form the list of optional criteria in addition to the one chosen for Level 1.

Figure 11.1. **Green certification scheme levels**

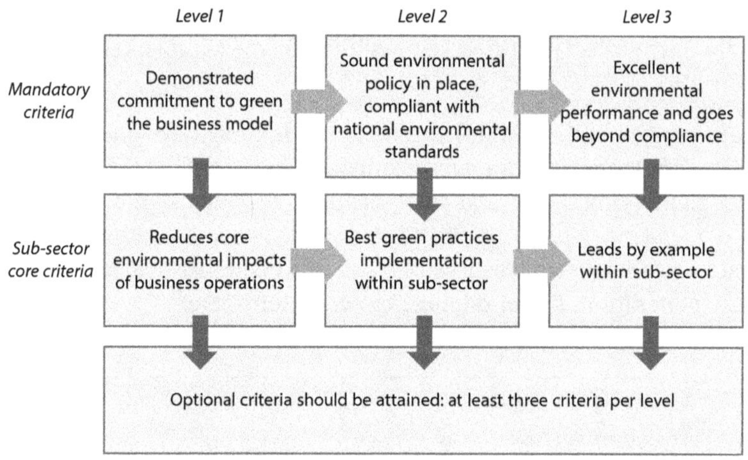

Mandatory criteria are applicable to all enterprises within the hospitality sector. Mandatory criteria are built around five pillars: EMS, water, waste and energy management and green purchasing. They should be classified in three certification levels, where the third level is the strictest.

Sub-sector core criteria should differ across the sub-sectors and, similarly to the mandatory criteria, should get stricter with the higher level of certification.

Sub-sector optional criteria should also be part of the scheme. The common list of optional criteria should be presented for the entire hospitality sector. A participating enterprise would need to choose at least three criteria from the list of optional criteria for Level 1, six for Level 2 and nine for Level 3 (if an enterprise already attained Level 1, it should maintain the optional criteria selected for this level and choose three new optional criteria to attain Level 2). Another possibility for an enterprise to add optional criteria could be to select from the list of mandatory or sub-sector core criteria of the higher level. For example, if an enterprise is wishing to obtain Level 1 certification, it can choose optional criteria from the list of Level 2 mandatory or sub-sector core criteria. This, however, will not be possible for enterprises applying for Level 3 certification.

Combining all three types of criteria allows the certification scheme to address the specifics of businesses within each hospitality sub-sector. The specific level should be considered attained if the GTA accreditation board judges that an enterprise fulfilled all the criteria for that level, based on the audit assessment results and documents provided by the applicant.

Table 11.1 presents an extensive list of suggested mandatory, sub-sector core and optional criteria. They are based on the certification standards of the Green Hospitality Awards programme, the Green Key programme and the Sustainable Tourism and are adapted to the Georgian context. Some enterprises in the hospitality sector might have already undertaken measures corresponding to several criteria (e.g. double-glazed windows) to save money or comply with local or national regulations.

Mandatory criteria should be universal for the entire hospitality sector and be based on Georgian environmental legislation. The highest level should go well beyond the environmental standards. In addition to the five pillars (EMS, water, waste and energy management and green purchasing), the third level could include criteria addressing environmental education within local communities.

The criteria differentiation for hospitality sub-sectors should evolve around the main business activity of an enterprise. For hotels, hostels and guest houses – providing accommodation, for restaurants, cafes and bars – catering, and for eco-tourism – outdoor activities.

Hotels

Hotels are the largest accommodation providers within the hospitality sector in Georgia. The criteria for this sub-sector cover a bigger variety of aspects than for hostels and guest houses. In general, hotels use more energy, water and other resources and produce more waste. Additionally, they usually offer catering services, which should also be addressed when setting the criteria.

Hostels and guest houses

The core sub-sector criteria need to include some requirements for premises. For example, double glazed windows for new buildings, well insulated doors, and other heat conservation measures.

Restaurants, cafes and bars

The business operations of restaurants, cafes and bars concentrate on food and beverage provision to consumers. Specific criteria for this sub-sector should address food waste disposal as well as one-time use food packaging for deliveries and take-outs (where applicable).

Eco-tourism providers

Since 2009, several projects on eco-tourism have already been implemented by the GTA. The GTA should work closely with the Agency of Protected Areas to set the eco-tourism criteria. It should build on the results achieved by the projects "Sustainable Tourism Development in Protected Areas" (2009) and "Enhancing Sustainability of Tourism Development in Protected Areas of Georgia" (2010), which recommended increased involvement of the local population in the development of sustainable tourism products in protected areas, environmental and traditional livelihood education, and improved marketing of sustainable tourism potential in Georgia.

In general, to attain the sub-sector core criteria eco-tourism providers should focus on:

- demonstrating that the main principles of eco-tourism are established and closely followed (explained in written document such as an eco-tourism guide)
- demonstrating the knowledge of natural and cultural heritage of the operating area and conveying this knowledge to customers
- contributing to conservation of the local natural capital and environment
- promoting the conservation and recycling principles to customers.

Conclusion

As tourism in Georgia continues to increase, and interest in green tourism continues to rise, there is a strong argument for establishing a green certification scheme in Georgia's hospitality sector. The use of a green certification scheme for SMEs in the hospitality sector provides benefits to both enterprises and consumers. As consumers become more environmentally conscious, there is a substantive demand for hospitality service providers, whether accommodation, adventure, or catering, to provide greener options. Being accredited with the green certification label and listed on a central website can help direct consumers to those businesses. The increased market share gained can help to offset the short term costs of investing in greener practices. Having different levels of accreditation helps ensure wide uptake, by allowing SMEs to target the level of accreditation that is feasible. In keeping with this, it's vital that achieving green certification makes commercial sense – the costs of achieving it cannot outweigh the potential benefits.

Table 11.1. **Green certification scheme: criteria by level**

Sub-sector/ criteria	Level 1	Level 2	Level 3
Mandatory criteria	• EMS documentation, including a signed environmental declaration and stated policy is published and displayed for customers. • Core legislative national and local requirements are complied with. • Environmental/green co-ordinator is appointed and trained. • Environmental/green file is created. The file contains information on green actions conducted by an enterprise. • Data on environmental impacts of business (waste, water and energy use) is collected and monitored. • Overall review of business is conducted and possible environmental actions and improvements are identified. • Waste separation programme is identified. • Only waste collectors with valid permits are used. • Active process is in place to identify water leaks. • Water flows from showers, toilets, wash basins are measured (where applicable). • The list of major energy using equipment is in place. • All lights in use are listed, including their type, class, wattage and estimated time in use annually. • The enterprise understands how heating and cooling is distributed throughout the building. • Green/sustainable purchasing policy is in place.	• All mandatory Level 1 criteria are complied with. • EMS documentation is complete, comprehensive, well presented with detailed benchmarking information. • Green certificate is displayed in a public area of the business. • All legislative national and local environmental requirements are complied with. • Data on environmental impacts of business (waste, water and energy use) are analysed and presented annually to the GTA accreditation board. • Steps are taken to minimise waste throughout the property and are documented (including reducing waste packaging from suppliers). • E-mail and internet are used for the majority of communications with customers. • Staff are trained to turn equipment off when it is not required. • Waste separation programme is implemented. • Public pathways outside the premises are kept free of litter. • All identified water leaks are treated on the premises. • The list of all energy using equipment is in place. • Total water consumption is registered at least bi-annually.	• All mandatory Level 1 and 2 criteria are complied with. • An enterprise goes beyond legislative national and local environmental requirements. • Analysis of data on environmental impacts of business (waste, water and energy use) is used to go beyond compliance. • Energy use is registered at least monthly. • Any new energy-using equipment is purchased based on best energy efficiency standards. • Suppliers are selected according to their environmental policy. • All employees are trained and aware of enterprises' green practices and demonstrate their knowledge where applicable. • Total water consumption is registered at least monthly. • All wastewater is treated. • Hazardous waste (batteries, fluo compact bulbs, paint, chemicals, etc.) are secured in separate containers and brought to an approved reception facility.

Table 11.1. **Green certification scheme: criteria by level** *(continued)*

Sub-sector/ criteria	Level 1	Level 2	Level 3
Hotels	• Staff are trained not to exceed recommended amounts of detergent and disinfectant indicated on the package. • Guests are given opportunity to separate waste according to local systems. • Adequate information on how to help the business save water is provided to guests. • Regular inspection and assessment of air-conditioning systems is in place. • All windows in rooms have an appropriate high degree of thermal insulation (except where planning restrictions apply). • If heating or air conditioning does not switch off automatically when windows are open, easily visible information is provided reminding the guests to close window if heating or air conditioning is on. • If there is no automatic switch off (or electronic key card) for lights in the room, easily visible information is provided to guests asking them to turn off the light when leaving the room. • 50% of all light bulbs within the property are energy efficient. • Maintenance and servicing of boilers are carried out at least annually. • Toilets are managed so that there are no leaks. • Legislation regarding polluting elements within enterprise's' premises is respected. • Organic food is identified and promoted on all menus.	• All sub-sector core Level 1 criteria are complied with. • Extensive annual report on the environmental activities of the business is produced. • The use of "one-use" or "single-portion" packaging for food items is minimised. • Unless required by law, none of the "one-portion" or "one-use" toiletries disposable products are used in rooms. • Towel and linen reuse programmes are in place, and advisory information to guests is visibly displayed. • External heating appliances operate on a zero-carbon output basis. • Any new boiler (heat generator) purchased within the businesses has a high level of efficiency. • Toilets are either dual flush or steps are taken to reduce the volume of water in the cisterns. • Efficiency of existing boiler(s) (heat generator) complies with strict efficiency standards. • Any newly installed heating of air conditioning system is designed so that it turns off if windows are opened in guest bedrooms. • Timers and controls are in place to avoid continuous operation of pool water features. • 65% of all light bulbs within the property are energy efficient.	• All sub-sector core Level 1 and 2 criteria are complied with. • Air conditioning in bedrooms switches off automatically when windows are open. • "One-use" or "single-portion" packaging for food items is not used. • 80% of all light bulbs within the property are energy efficient. • 100% of all light bulbs likely to be turned on for more than 5 hours are energy efficient. • Leisure centres' swimming pools have thermal covers in use nightly and when the centre is closed for use.
Hostels and guest houses	• Double-glazed windows are used in new building(s). • Energy saving light bulbs are used where possible. • Legislation regarding polluting elements within enterprise's' premises is respected. • Buildings are well insulated. • Toilets are managed so that there are no leaks.	• All sub-sector core Level 1 criteria are complied with. • External heating appliances do not use fossil fuels. • Energy efficient bulbs are used in all areas where bulbs are on for more than 5 hours daily. • Towel reuse programme is in place. • An enterprise choose energy efficient refrigerators, dishwashers, washing machines and office equipment. • 50% of all light bulbs within the property are energy efficient. • Use of individual toiletries is restricted. • Toilets are either dual flush or steps are taken to reduce the volume of water in the cisterns.	• All sub-sector core Level 1 and 2 criteria are complied with. • Linen reuse programme is in place. • Low-flow showers are in use. • 75% of all light bulbs within the property are energy efficient. • "One-use" or "single-portion" packaging for food items is not used.

Table 11.1. **Green certification scheme: criteria by level** *(continued)*

Sub-sector/ criteria	Level 1	Level 2	Level 3
Restaurants, cafes and bars	• Organic food is identified and promoted on all menus. • Refrigerators are positioned and regulated according to energy saving principles. • Toilets are managed so that there are no leaks.	• All sub-sector core Level 1 criteria are complied with. • "One-use" or "single-portion" packaging for food items and any disposable food service items use is minimised. • All new refrigerators, dishwashers and cooking equipment is purchased based on energy efficiency principles. • Energy efficient bulbs are in use in all areas where bulbs are on for more than 5 hours daily. • Toilets are either dual flush or steps are taken to reduce the volume of water in the cisterns.	• All sub-sector core Level 1 and 2 criteria are complied with. • "One-use" or "single-portion" packaging for food items and any disposable food service items are not in use.
Eco-tourism providers	• Environmental and cultural awareness campaign is designed and customers are advised. • Knowledge of natural and cultural heritage of the operating area is demonstrated and conveyed to customers. • Memorable interpretative materials that help raise awareness of Georgia's environmental assets are promoted to customers.	• All sub-sector core criteria Level 1 are complied with. • Environmental and cultural awareness campaign is fully implemented. • The enterprise contributes to conservation of the local natural capital and environment. • External heating appliances do not use fossil fuels. • Energy efficient bulbs are in use in all areas where bulbs are on for more than 5 hours daily.	• All sub-sector core Level 1 and 2 criteria are complied with. • Conservation and recycling principles are promoted to customers, partner hospitality establishments. • An enterprise is actively promoting its practices on conservation of the local natural capital and environment.
Optional criteria	**Environmental management system, green purchasing, biodiversity, culture and social responsibility:** • At least 70% of all chemicals, detergents, soaps, toiletries etc. should be environmentally friendly (certified, if possible) and are fully biodegradable. • Bicycles are provided for customers. • Guest comment cards or satisfaction questionnaires include environmental questions and feedback questions on environmental performance of the enterprise. • Disinfectants are used only where necessary in order to comply with hygiene requirements. • At least some of such practices as car-free and public transportation promotion, and promotion of "carbon free" packages to guests are introduced. • Suppliers are asked for their environmental policies, and supplier selection is based on their environmental performance.		

Table 11.1. **Green certification scheme: criteria by level** *(continued)*

Sub-sector/ criteria	Level 1	Level 2	Level 3
Optional criteria *(cont.)*	**Waste management:** • The use of bottled water is minimised. • Cooking oil is purchased in bulk. • Battery collection point is provided for visitors. • Recycled paper is used. • Reusable printer cartridges are used. • Composting system on site for all food waste is in place. **Water management:** • Rain water is saved and used for non-drinking purposes. • Taps in washbasins have reduced flows. • Toilets have reduced flows/timers installed. • Recycled water is collected and used for non-sanitary and non-drinking purposes. • Washing machines used in the accommodation are managed with water use reduction techniques. • Low-impact chemical free cleaners such as microfiber are used. **Energy management:** • Building(s) is/are well insulated. • Boilers and water tanks are well insulated. • Windows are at least double glazed. • Green electricity is used (if available). • Automatic light controls are in place. • Heating is thermostatically controlled. • A share of electricity is generated through renewable energy sources (at least 20%). • The building has insulation above the minimal national requirements, to ensure a significant reduction of energy consumption. • Business chooses energy efficient refrigerators, dishwashers, washing machines and office equipment. • Automatic systems which turn the lights off when guests leave their rooms are installed in at least 80% of the guest rooms. • Unnecessary outside lights are turned off automatically. • Heating/cooling is zoned into different areas, depending on the use of the premises, each controlled separately by a thermostat. • Heat recovery system is in place for any of the following categories: refrigeration systems, ventilation/air handling, washing machines, dishwashers, swimming pool(s), sanitary waste water. • The temperature in every room is individually regulated. • Sensors/timers are installed in all areas to control lighting.		

References

Georgian National Tourism Administration (2014), *Georgian tourism in figures: Structure and industry data*, https://gnta.ge/wp-content/uploads/2014/08/eng-4print10.pdf.

Honey, M. and Rome, A. (2001), *Protecting Paradise: Certification Programs for Sustainable Tourism and Ecotourism*, Institute for Policy Studies, https://portals.iucn.org/library/node/26145.

OECD (2015), *Promoting better environmental performance of small and medium-sized enterprises in Armenia*, Pilot project report, Greening Economies in the Eastern Neighbourhood programme, Organisation for Economic Co-operation and Development, Paris, www.oecd.org/environment/outreach/SME-greening-country-pilot-report-Armenia-en.pdf.

OECD (2014), SME Policy Index. Eastern Partner Countries: Assessing the implementation of small business act for Europe, Organisation for Economic Co-operation and Development, Paris.

ORGANISATION FOR ECONOMIC CO-OPERATION AND DEVELOPMENT

The OECD is a unique forum where governments work together to address the economic, social and environmental challenges of globalisation. The OECD is also at the forefront of efforts to understand and to help governments respond to new developments and concerns, such as corporate governance, the information economy and the challenges of an ageing population. The Organisation provides a setting where governments can compare policy experiences, seek answers to common problems, identify good practice and work to co-ordinate domestic and international policies.

The OECD member countries are: Australia, Austria, Belgium, Canada, Chile, the Czech Republic, Denmark, Estonia, Finland, France, Germany, Greece, Hungary, Iceland, Ireland, Israel, Italy, Japan, Korea, Latvia, Luxembourg, Mexico, the Netherlands, New Zealand, Norway, Poland, Portugal, the Slovak Republic, Slovenia, Spain, Sweden, Switzerland, Turkey, the United Kingdom and the United States. The European Union takes part in the work of the OECD.

OECD Publishing disseminates widely the results of the Organisation's statistics gathering and research on economic, social and environmental issues, as well as the conventions, guidelines and standards agreed by its members.

OECD PUBLISHING, 2, rue André-Pascal, 75775 PARIS CEDEX 16
(97 2018 03 1 P) ISBN 978-92-64-29317-5 – 2018

www.ingramcontent.com/pod-product-compliance
Lightning Source LLC
Chambersburg PA
CBHW061217240926
51846CB00006B/1252